I Remember
ARTHUR ASHE

I Remember
ARTHUR ASHE

*Memories of a True Tennis Pioneer
and Champion of Social Causes
by the People Who Knew Him*

MIKE TOWLE

**Cumberland House
Nashville, Tennessee**

Published by Cumberland House Publishing, Inc., 431 Harding Industrial Drive, Nashville, TN 37211

Cover design by Gore Studio, Inc.
Text design by Mary Sanford

Library of Congress Cataloging-in-Publication Data
I remember Arthur Ashe : memories of a true tennis pioneer and champion of social causes by the people who knew him / [compiled by] Mike Towle.
    p. cm.
  Includes bibliographical references and index.
  ISBN 1-58182-149-2 (hardcover : alk. paper)
   1. Ashe, Arthur. 2. Tennis players--United States--Biography. 3. African American tennis players--Biography. I. Title: Arthur Ashe. II. Towle, Mike.

GV994.A7 I22 2001
796.342'092--dc21
[B]
                                        00-065920

Printed in the United States of America
1 2 3 4 5 6 7—06 05 04 03 02 01

To Holley and Andrew

Contents

PREFACE

In setting out to do this book, I wasn't sure what I would find. I never met Arthur Ashe and never even actually covered much tennis in my days as a full-time sportswriter for the *Fort Worth Star-Telegram* and *The National*. Even had I covered a significant amount of tennis during those years, my sportswriting era came too late for me to have had a chance to see Arthur Ashe in action as one of the world's top players.

Arthur had retired from tennis at about the same time I was graduating from college and beginning a four-year stint as an active duty U.S. Army officer. I didn't get into full-time sportswriting until 1982, by which time Arthur was retired from the ranks of active tennis player and perched in a broadcaster's booth for ABC and HBO, commentating on tennis.

One way of life in the world of reporting is chasing down and exploring subjects with which we have had no previous exposure. Such was the case with this author and Arthur. Unlike attorneys and comedians, reporters often don't know the answers before they ask the questions. Ignorance can be a wonderful source of inspiration for reporters, writers, and authors to pursue their subject matter, which helps explain why I chose to put together this book about tennis great Arthur Ashe. I knew enough about Ashe to know that I did not know everything about him, even seven years after his death from AIDS-related pneumonia in February 1993. There was so much more I wanted to know about him, beginning with the premise that he was the first prominent African-American male in a white man's tennis world and continuing on through the causes he tackled, such as apartheid in South Africa. Who was this gentle, incredibly articulate man who was able to shake worldwide politics and prejudices in a manner so dignified and, at times, under-stated? We knew in bits and pieces what his legacy was shaping up to be, so the question to resolve then became not what his legacy was, but why it was what it was.

In diving into the subject of Arthur Ashe's life, and death, I started at square one with nary a starting point for credible contacts to be interviewed for this book. I was never a tennis beat writer and certainly not a tennis junkie. Early on in this project, I turned to several people to help me find my way. Some of these people I knew, such as Frank Deford, under whom I toiled as a reporter at *The National* and who had since blossomed from acquaintance to friend; and some I didn't know, such as Randy Walker at the United States Tennis Association, who was generous time and again in providing me with telephone numbers and e-mail addresses for a number of sources quoted in this book. Ditto for Greg Sharko at the Association of Tennis Professionals, as well as agent Jeremy Steindecker.

As with all of the books I have been involved with in this burgeoning series of "I Remember" books, there were a number of potential interviewees contacted by me who either declined my request to be interviewed or wouldn't/couldn't contact me in response to messages left by me. That's why I am especially grateful to the people who allowed me to impose on their time long enough to grant me interviews that were insightful and enlightening. Thank you Donald Dell, Stan Smith, Pam Shriver, Rodney Harmon, Willis Thomas, Harry Marmion, Chris Beck, DD Eisenberg, Seth Abraham, Bud Collins, Frank Deford, Eliot Teltscher, Tom Okker, Judge Robert Kelleher, Dennis Ralston, Gladys Heldman, and Nick Bollettieri.

As always, a hearty thanks goes to my publisher Ron Pitkin at Cumberland House for his continued faith in this "I Remember" series, and to my editor Mary Sanford for putting plenty of spit and polish to this project.

My wife, Holley, and son, Andrew, patiently persevered as I sequestered myself for hours on end in completing this project, interviewing, transcribing, editing, writing, cutting, and pasting into the wee hours week after week. Thank you from the bottom of my heart.

Thanks, of course, to my Lord and Savior, Jesus Christ, for keeping me going through thick and thin.

INTRODUCTION

Arthur Ashe was forty-nine years old when he passed away on February 6, 1993, a victim of pneumonia. Nearly six thousand people attended Ashe's funeral. Among the mourners were former New York City mayor David Dinkins, Virginia governor Doug Wilder and Rainbow Coalition chairman Jesse Jackson, all of whom Ashe had been able to call friend. Former Atlanta mayor and U.N. ambassador Andrew Young delivered the eulogy. The name dropping could go on and on, and that's even without counting the many from the world of tennis who mourned Ashe's death.

That's the way it was with Ashe, a tennis champion whose Grand Slam victories in the U.S. Open, Australian Open, and at Wimbledon only begin to tell his story. Ashe was born in the segregated South and took up tennis at age seven, a move that ultimately brought an even more focused attention to the fact that the color of his skin was black. Even moreso than golf, tennis has long been a predominantly white man's sport with very little in the way of multiracial opportunity. Make a list of sports "suitable" for a black youth growing up during the fifties and sixties, and tennis goes to the bottom. That's what makes Ashe's story so unique. At age seven he took up a sport that few others of his race had and then not only reached the pinnacle of his sport, but used his success in that arena as a springboard to having a prominent voice on issues that went well beyond sports.

Ashe's life story is centered around tennis, but the outer circle of his influence comprises a huge area. Arthur Ashe: statesman, author, activist, husband, father, teacher, politician, barrier breaker, traveler, student, champion, board director, television commentator, trusted friend, protester. That's not a complete list, but it is a quick glimpse of a bold and dignified man who happened to be an African American with an ability to reach out beyond cultural, racial, and international barriers.

Ashe once said that if he had been remembered only as a tennis player, he would have considered himself a failure. But he was far from a failure as testified to by many of the people whose lives he touched in one form or fashion.

I Remember
ARTHUR ASHE

THE VIRGINIAN

Arthur Ashe was born in 1943 in the segregated Southern city of Richmond, Virginia, to Arthur and Mattie Ashe. In his book *Poetry in Motion*, Ashe remembers his childhood days as happy ones, in part because his working middle-class family lived near Brook Park, a park for African Americans that included tennis courts and a swimming pool. Arthur Sr. worked as a maintenance man as well as park policeman, the latter a position that sometimes put him at odds with other blacks who pushed the envelope of civility sometimes by riding bikes where they weren't supposed to or breaking soft-drink bottles and leaving the pieces behind for someone else to clean up.

Tennis was a popular recreational pastime throughout much of Richmond, and not just for whites only. It was on those tennis courts in Richmond that young Arthur Ashe, skinny and frail, took up a game that would become a passion as well as his pass, a platform from which he would emerge and mature as a political activist fighting against ignorance and prejudice. His family upbringing cloaked him in traditional values and a lifelong infatuation with all things educational and intellectually challenging.

In order to become a good role model as an adult, Arthur at a young age had to have strong mentors of his own. One was his stern yet caring father, who would later break down in tears when his son won the first U.S. Open. Another was Dr. Robert Walter Johnson Jr., an African American from nearby Lynchburg who, through tennis, instilled in Ashe and other tennis-playing black youths virtues such as comportment, politeness, focus, and discipline. These were among the qualities that years later Arthur would pass along to apprentices such as Rodney Harmon, another black tennis player who came out of Richmond, as well as those thousands of youths he met and mentored at the many tennis clinics he gave over the years. Dr. Johnson rarely had trouble getting a captive audience with his players. Long drives in a van to tennis tournaments took care of that.

Through his prowess early on as a tennis prodigy, Arthur had doors into the white man's world opened for him in Richmond and beyond, but he never left his African-American heritage completely behind. If he needed a reminder of that, as a youth all he had to do was board a public bus and see the white line on the floor reminding blacks to step to the rear or try to see if he could get into any area country clubs to play tennis there. Years later his quiet dignity would evolve into controlled outrage when confronting such issues as apartheid in South Africa and unsportsmanlike conduct among his tennis peers.

*One of Ashe's early tennis-playing friends was Washington,
D.C., native* **Willis Thomas** *who often played doubles with
Ashe during their days traveling the junior circuit. Thomas was
a good junior player, but not good enough to join Ashe in helping to break down the color barrier in men's tennis. Thomas quit
competitive tennis after he turned eighteen, but has kept his hand
in the game over the years, coaching such talented African
Americans as Rodney Harmon and Zina Garrison:*

We were ten years old when I first met him. This was on the
American Tennis Association Tour. In the early days, up
until about age fourteen, it seems we would always end up in
the finals and Arthur would always end up beating me.
There was one time that I beat him in the first set and was
leading 5-3 in the second when it started pouring down rain.
It was on a Sunday when everything was a weekend tournament and everyone was to go back to work on Monday, so it
was decided to flip a coin to determine our match and he
won that too. I was always kind of unlucky when it came to
playing him.

He was like any other kid, but a little different in a way
in that he always had his eye on the future and kind of knew
where he wanted to go, which was unusual for a kid of that
age. From the time he was thirteen he said that he was going
to go to UCLA, and I would say, "Hey, you live a long way
from California, how are you going to go to UCLA?" UCLA?
We would just laugh at him. After all, this was California in
the early 1960s, and you're talking about a whole different
world. Going to California was like going to another country because it's so far out there, and in those days you didn't
see black folks going to colleges like that except for maybe
one or two guys playing football or basketball. But he had

great vision and knew how to set his mind so that he could see his goals. That's how he played tennis and that made him a very difficult person to play. He didn't show much emotion because he knew what he had to do, and I think that carried over to his life in general as well. It was intimidating a bit.

I was a much better athlete than Arthur was, but I didn't have the same power mentally that he did. It was intimidating, even though he was sort of a small, scraggly kid. He didn't look like much. We used to tease him a lot about being a little arrogant, which I guess goes along with the territory of being such a good player. One time we were in New York at Forest Hills playing in the Eastern Junior Boys—we were about fifteen then—and he ended up losing to a kid whose name I think was Billy Brown. And it was a pretty one-sided loss, something like 2 and 3. When we got to Kalamazoo a few weeks later, Arthur went out and beat that boy, 0 and 0. That's what I remember about him. That's when I knew this guy was good—to go and beat a guy 0 and 0 just a couple weeks after losing by quite a bit to this same kid.

We were definitely much in the minority in these events as two blacks. But the thing about Arthur was that he was one of those individuals who could walk both sides of the fence. Blacks liked him and so did whites. I know when they had several parties for the players in Kalamazoo, they would get some local girls to come in for the dance and Arthur would go to the dance while some of the other fellows would just walk into downtown Kalamazoo. He felt he belonged, and that's what it takes.

☙❧

Ashe grew up in Richmond, Virginia, which, though segregated for many years, crossed the color line in embracing tennis as a favorite recreational pursuit for blacks and whites alike. Ashe also had the stability of growing up in a household that espoused traditional values such as hard work and honesty, as well as courtesy, as he himself explained:

Drummed into me above all, by my dad, by the whole family, was that without your good name, you would be nothing. When some old black lady, maybe your grandmother or maybe a dignified domestic on her way home from cleaning the white people's houses, saw you or any other black boy doing something wrong, there was one expression she would use that you did not want to hear. It meant you were letting everybody down—your friends, your family, your history. And that expression was, "Boy, you should be ashamed of yourself." Lord, the weight those words carried.[1]

❧

*Although **Thomas** wasn't one of Ashe's neighbors growing up, he got to know the future Wimbledon champion well, spending summers driving up and down the East Coast with him participating in prestigious junior events as well as the occasional national event in which they were the only blacks in an otherwise all-white world:*

I grew up in Washington, D.C. But the black circuit we played on in those days was played up and down the East Coast, from North Carolina all the way up to New York City. We competed on weekends.

Richmond was segregated for a long time. You know his

7

Much of Ashe's career was associated with his participation in Davis Cup play, both as a player and as a captain. (Jim Osborne, AP/Wide World Photos)

father was a park policeman, and because of his job he locked up a lot of blacks, and so he was kind of known as an instrument of the white man down there. He was caught in the middle. As far as blacks go, you could say that they (the

Ashes) had a house on sort of the higher end and they lived right on the park. Arthur probably grew up also knowing whites and that probably helped him from the standpoint that he didn't see white when he was playing a white player. It was a little more normal for him than it would have been for most other blacks. I think his being black in a traditionally white man's sport drove him, but I don't think that drive was as deep as it was for some of the other black players.

We played a lot of doubles in those early years. We used to tour in the summer. We were some of the first blacks to be playing some of these tournaments, like up at Forest Hills or the Western Junior Boys. We were good doubles partners. Even at that time, he was very steady, a great player to have beside you because his ground strokes were so good and he would make you look good. A lot of players at that time didn't have anywhere to go—you only played tennis in the summertime. I would play tennis maybe April through August, then I would put the tennis racket in the closet and concentrate on playing other sports, such as basketball. I never played tennis in the wintertime. When Arthur got good was when he moved to (Florida, to be in Nick Bollettieri's tennis academy)—he jumped ahead of everybody, because he now was playing tennis twelve months out of the year.

The only time I ever saw Dr. (Robert) Johnson (Ashe's youth coach) get into Arthur was when we were playing Clark Graebner and Warren Dane. We played them one year in a doubles quarterfinal, it was either Kalamazoo or the Western. It was one of my better days playing but Arthur did not play well that day. Anyway, Dr. Johnson told us, "When you go out there, hit everything to Warren Dane." Of course, as it turned out, every ball we hit was to Clark Graebner. We didn't follow instructions very well. Now as a coach, I can look back and know how Dr. Johnson felt. If we had won the match, it would have been a huge thing for black folks, so now I can understand why he got so upset. I think we were kind of awed ourselves during the match because we were playing the top team. Of course, I think a lot of the reason it appeared like we were hitting it to him was because he (Graebner) was so aggressive on his side of the net going for almost every ball.

We were a little Jekyll and Hyde. We teamed up early on and were successful in the black program. There might have been a lot of times when Arthur wanted to play with someone else because I was a nonconformer kind of person. I sometimes wouldn't pay too much attention to what someone said and Arthur would follow me and we'd both get into trouble. I just wasn't as serious as he was, but we ended up playing about three or four years together, so I guess that was good enough. Actually, I didn't realize he was going to be a great player until he beat that kid 0 and 0 in Kalamazoo. Then I knew. And there was no name calling at the tournament because of our being black. In fact, the people kind of embraced him. People will recognize talent, no matter what color you were, and they saw that in Arthur and embraced him.

When I started coaching in the early seventies, I said I'll start by going to join the USTA. Just like now, to join the professional organization, you had to take a test and that sort of thing. In this area of the country, the testing was being conducted by a pro at the Country Club of Virginia in Richmond, the biggest country club in Richmond. So I signed up to take my test, and this was in the early seventies, but they wouldn't let me on the grounds of that country club. No blacks allowed.

I always went a different direction than Arthur. He always went the straight and narrow and I went the other way. But our paths always crossed. One time he came back to Richmond to play in a local tournament and I ended up playing him in the second round and actually won a game from him, so at least he didn't beat me 0 and 0. Our paths crossed even after that. I coached Rodney Harmon, and it seems Arthur was always around. Then I coached Zina Garrison and would still see Arthur around a lot.

I was more unpredictable than Arthur and I think that helped me with my coaching. I remember one year we were at Wimbledon and he wasn't playing anymore. He was doing commentary and I was coaching Zina then. We had talked years earlier about how he thought Zina could play at the net, and I said, "Arthur, Zina knows how to play at the net, my job is just trying to get her to come to the net." This was during Zina's best times as a player, just prior to her beating Martina (Navratilova) at the U.S. Open.

❧

One of Ashe's closest professional associates over the last twenty years of his life was **Christine (Chris) Beck,** *who also grew up playing the junior circuit in the fifties and early sixties, and now is active with the Arthur Ashe Youth Tennis Center in Philadelphia:*

Arthur and I had exactly the same birthday, day and year— July 10, 1943. I first met Arthur when we were teenagers competing in junior tennis tournaments. I was playing in a tournament in Wilmington, Delaware, one time and he and some players came up from Richmond. What I remember about that experience is that until then I had lived a pretty sheltered life and I still remember how horrified I was that he and the other African Americans from Richmond were not allowed to use the locker room in the club. That bowled me over. How could this be possible? I was good enough to compete on the national grass court circuit, which concluded at Forest Hills, but he was so much better than the skill level I was playing at.

It was a special experience to go to different areas of the country and meet new people and compete. Arthur obviously loved the sport of tennis, and one of the things he loved to talk about, in terms of the benefits of tennis for young people, was as an individual sport the life lessons you would learn. There is no timeout in tennis, no coaching (during matches)—you're out there on your own doing the best you can and learning to be fair with your line calls. Being self-reliant, and able to accept winning and losing. Those are certainly life skills. Certainly all of us who played junior tennis learned those things. Tennis players learn to grow up in a hurry and to be accountable.

⁂

Ashe had a number of protégés over the years who went on to make their mark on tennis's world stage, such as Yannick Noah, who Ashe "discovered" as a teenager in Cameroon. Another of Ashe's mentored players was **Rodney Harmon,** *who, like Arthur, had grown up in Richmond but a generation later. Harmon, now director of multicultural development for the United States Tennis Association (USTA), played collegiate tennis at the University of Tennessee and Southern Methodist University, making his most lasting mark in tennis when he*

*reached the quarterfinals of the 1982 U.S. Open before losing
to Jimmy Connors:*

I met him the first time at a park where I grew up in
Richmond. I was about eight years old and this was the late
sixties. When he won the U.S. Open in 1968, everyone in
Richmond was so happy about it and I can remember that.
He would come back and give clinics at the park. It was great
to be able to be out there with him, seeing him teach and so
forth. Tennis in our community has always been big and
always very popular. A lot of black people play tennis in
Richmond, and for Arthur to go on and do so well was phenomenal for us. Then in 1972 or 1973 I won an award from
American Express that honors the most promising player in
the country, and it was an award for which Arthur had nom-
inated me. That was great because I got to receive the award
at Forest Hills at the U.S. Open. It was a really great moment
for me.

From that point on, I would see Arthur every year
because we would have a WCT event in Richmond every
year and he would typically play in it. I was a ballboy and
would watch him. As I got a little older, when I was seventeen in fact, Arthur helped me to be able to go to Nick
Bollettieri's tennis academy. That was another great thing for
me because it gave me a chance to learn how to be a good
player. I had been playing tennis about two or three days a
week back in Richmond, and without having a chance to go
to the academy, I don't think I could have been the player I
wanted to be. I was ranked like fifteenth or sixteenth in the
country when I got down there and when I left after six
months there, I won the Easter Bowl and finished No. 3 in
the country for juniors. I won three national titles in doubles

and made it to the finals of the national tournament in Kalamazoo, and it was all because I got the opportunity thanks to Arthur, and Nick is such a great coach and such a great motivator. Arthur learned to play tennis at Brookfield Park in Richmond. But after Arthur left to go onto the tennis circuit, they ended up dismantling Brookfield, taking down all the nets and the lights and so forth. They then brought Brookfield's lights to Battery Park, which is right near my house and where I learned to play. It is maybe about five minutes away. I think it's now called the Arthur Ashe Tennis Center. I grew up basically three houses from the court, close enough to where I could look out my window and tell whether the courts were wet or dry. Basically, I spent my life at the courts. I loved to play, and the good thing about the park when I was growing up was that there was a great cross-section of people who would play there, to include doctors, lawyers, and accountants—all kinds of people—and these were people who were more concerned about you as a person than how well you played tennis. It was a very safe environment to grow up in, one that I wouldn't trade for anything in the world.

Arthur didn't come to the park that often, maybe once or twice a year because he was playing the tour by then and was very busy. Still, he helped me out a lot. Another time I transferred from the University of Tennessee to Southern Methodist University, and Arthur assisted me in making the transition by helping me with the cost of some of my tuition because, as mandated by NCAA rules, I had to sit out from tennis for a year after making the transfer. His deal was that I would only have to worry about paying him back if I didn't graduate. It was really important to him that I graduate, so I graduated. Dennis Ralston was the tennis coach at SMU then, and he had been one of the Davis Cup captains when Arthur was on the team. Arthur was friends with Dennis and he thought Dennis could help me a lot, and he did help me improve a lot. From there, Arthur just continued to help me with things as they came up.

⌀⟋⟍⟍⟍⟍⟍⟍⟋

When Ashe mentored others, it usually involved much more than just giving tennis tips. It was all about life's lessons, many of which he learned at a young age:

We were taught table manners and the strictest etiquette and that unshakable Oriental calm. But I also noticed that control was damn effective. Other players' fathers were always telling Dr. Johnson (Dr. Robert Johnson Jr., Ashe's childhood tennis coach), "My son was going to pieces. Your player never changed expression." Everybody stressed sportsmanship in the black tennis community, because the community was a creature of the black middle class. Doctors, teachers, morticians—image meant nothing to them. I envied players who could sling a racket and get away with it.[2]

⌀⟋⟍⟍⟍⟍⟍⟍⟋

Although veteran tennis journalist and television commentator **Bud Collins** *didn't get to know Ashe well until after Ashe had graduated from UCLA, they developed a mutual respect over the years to the point where Collins got to know the tennis player well and gained a good feel for the events of Ashe's past and upbringing. This was in a day and age when beat reporters and the athletes they covered were friends more than they were* *protagonists stuck on the opposite ends of a media frenzy that fostered mistrust:*

Arthur certainly evolved and matured over time. You know, he was a very serious kind of a guy because of his father. Education came first. His father was considered an Uncle Tom by many black people in Richmond. He believed that you were polite and that if you weren't wanted somewhere, then okay, you didn't go. He wanted his boys to be educated and he wanted them to be obedient, and he wanted them to work hard in school. What Arthur said to him was that he wanted to be a tennis player, and his father said to him, "Well, then you had better work and be the best tennis player that you can be or I'm not interested, and your school-work will not suffer because of it."

Arthur's father, Arthur Sr., was a marvelous man. I can remember that day when Arthur beat Okker in the 1968 U.S. Open—I did that telecast—I was on my way back to the press box to write my story and was going through a pas-sageway in the stadium and I saw Mr. Ashe standing there alone, weeping. I went over and said, "Mr. Ashe, is every-thing all right?" And he said, "Oh, God, yes, everything is wonderful. But when I think of that boy"—because Arthur was a very sickly child, apparently—"and how we almost lost him, and to come to this day . . ." He was so overcome, but he didn't want anybody to see him crying. I knew him well enough to go over and see if there was anything wrong, like if anybody had died or someone had said something deroga-tory to him about a black man winning the tournament.

ᏜᎷᎳᎴ

*As a native of Richmond, it was only natural for **Harmon** to follow Ashe's lead as a tennis-playing role model:*

Arthur was a role model because he was black and from my hometown, and he even grew up on the same side of Richmond that I grew up on, and my grandmother knew his mother, so my family knew his growing up. Then when we moved to the other side of Richmond, we moved right next to these tennis courts and my brother, Burrell, started playing tennis first. Once I started playing, I got hooked because tennis is the type of sport that will hook you before you really know it. Once Burrell started playing, I started playing, and having someone like Arthur you could look up to—someone who was so successful and obviously so much a citizen of the world—was something that meant a lot to me. He was different from anybody else in Richmond because he had traveled so much, and he had such a different view of the world and it was such a joy to talk about it with him. He would talk about things he had seen in places like Paris or Australia, or about any place I had dreamed about or wanted to go. And, again, seeing him without an entourage was so meaningful, especially compared to now when it seems like everyone has an entourage to include a bodyguard, handlers, coaches, etc. That wasn't his thing.

He would tell me, "You know, you can learn something from everyone around you if you just take the time to open your ears and listen. You've got to realize that the Lord blessed you with two ears and only one mouth, so He wants you to listen twice as much as you talk." If you grew up in the South like I did, that was the kind of thing that you heard a lot. I was raised in a household that was fairly strict, where it was always "Yes, Ma'am," or "Yes, Sir," and Arthur came from the same sort of set-up. His dad, Mr. Ashe, was really tough. As a matter of fact, when I was young, Arthur's dad was the policeman at the courts where I grew up, at Battery Park. He had this rule where he didn't want kids riding their bikes down the hill and through the park, where kids were playing, and he didn't want these kids to get hit while they were playing. But people would try to ride their bikes through and Mr. Ashe would confiscate their bikes. You didn't want him to do that. I never had mine confiscated, but I watched as other people lost theirs. I was down there at the park to play tennis, not to ride my bike.

I was fanatical about the amount of time I played tennis there. That was really my life and still is, and my life is really involved in tennis. I still try to play almost every day. But the bike was not my thing. Mr. Ashe was a very tough man. I can remember one year when Arthur came home to Richmond—and it might have been right after he won at Wimbledon—he came back for the WCT Tournament they had in Richmond, and for many years Arthur's dad had helped them put the court down for the indoor event. It was an indoor rug kind of a court. There were a lot of people in Richmond who were actually kind of angry about this, wondering why after Arthur had won at Wimbledon his dad was still having to do workman things like putting down the court—they thought he should be in the stands relaxing now because Arthur had been so successful. The bottom line, basically, was that Mr. Ashe still enjoyed doing this for himself.

Keep in mind that when Arthur grew up, Richmond was a segregated city and it could be a tough place to be for an African American, such as there being a park where he couldn't play. On the other hand, there were some white people in Richmond who had helped Arthur a lot, and one of the people running the WCT event at that time was one of those men who had been very helpful to Arthur while he was growing up, and Mr. Ashe wasn't going to turn his back on this guy just because Arthur had won Wimbledon. He didn't mind continuing to help someone who had helped his own son out many years before.

There was a lot of discipline in their household and I think that carried over into Arthur's tennis because he was able to work hard and deal with moving away from home early on. Moved up to St. Louis and spent a lot of summers down in Lynchburg. He made a lot of sacrifices to be a good player.

૭૦૦૦૦૭

2

TENNIS ACE

When making a list of the greatest male tennis players of all time, Arthur Ashe isn't necessarily the first past champion who comes to mind. But whereas Ashe didn't set any records for Grand Slam events won during his career, his accomplishments are many and varied. They form the foundation in defining the greatness of a man who far transcended his sport, yet they show him to be a great player who won at many different levels and in a great variety of settings.

Ashe grew up in Richmond, Virginia, learning tennis from part-time tennis coach Ron Charity, who then introduced Arthur to Lynchburg's Dr. Robert Johnson, who also coached the great African-American tennis player Althea Gibson. In becoming Ashe's mentor, Johnson took Ashe and other promising young black players to matches around the country featuring the nation's top junior players. As a high school senior, Ashe eventually moved to Saint Louis to stay at the home of a tennis official. He did this so he would be closer to the action of top tournaments.

In enrolling at UCLA after he graduated from high school, Ashe lived out a promise he had made when he was thirteen years old. At UCLA, Ashe's tennis career started to

Ashe strains for an overhead return against Phil Dent in the 1978 French Open. (AP/Wide World Photos)

blossom. In 1963, while a junior, he was named to the U.S. Davis Cup team, the first African-American male so designated. He then won the NCAA men's singles championship in 1965 while leading the Bruins to the NCAA team title.

Almost everywhere he went, Ashe stood out not only for his uniquely hard-hitting style of play but also for being the only black in a sport wallpapered with white faces and white tennis outfits. But he rarely wavered. In 1968 he became the only person ever, black or white, to win the U.S. amateur tennis championship and the U.S. Open in the same year. Ashe added more Grand Slam titles at the Australian Open (in 1970) and at Wimbledon, where in 1975 he achieved one of the greatest upsets in the sport's history, beating number one–ranked Jimmy Connors in a somewhat one-sided final, 6-1, 6-1, 5-7, 6-4. Mixed in among these and other singles titles was Davis Cup play, where Ashe simply was superb. He won twenty-eight of the thirty-four Davis Cup matches in which he played, spread over fifteen years.

A year after suffering a heart attack in 1979 at age thirty-six, Ashe retired from competitive tennis. His final record as a professional: 818 wins and 260 losses. All told, he won fifty-one titles.

⌒⟋⟍⟍⟍⟍⟍⟍⟋

Although Ashe was alone in his sport in terms of being the lone black man competing at the highest level of tennis, he was anything but alone in his life. He had a number of close friends who also happened to be rivals in a sport that fostered camaraderie as much as it did competition. One of his best friends as well as rival through the last thirty years of Ashe's life was **Stan Smith,** *who at times was Ashe's doubles partner as well as spiritual mentor:*

He was a difficult player to play against because he had two different parts to his career. In his original career, he was purely a slasher. I really believe he was a smart player, but he would just go for shots, and if you were his opponent you really felt like you didn't have control of the match. If he played well, he'd win; and if he played poorly, you'd win. He would dictate the issue. He'd either hit the fence or hit winners. He had a great backhand, but his forehand was a little shaky. Also, he had a great serve and could volley pretty well. Then he went through a period where he hurt his leg and came back in the last three or four years, to include winning Wimbledon (in 1975). By this time, he was playing much more intelligently. He also got very, very fit and became more aggressive in his tactics. Not that he would hit the ball harder or go for shots more, but he tried a few more things and played percentages a bit better.

Arthur often took advantage of his athleticism and would come to the net more. He would put pressure on guys by coming to the net and playing aggressively instead of just ripping balls from his heels, trying to hit winners all the time. A great match that obviously exemplified his maturity in tactics was when he beat Connors at Wimbledon. Instead of hitting the ball as hard as he could, Arthur would slice the ball out wide. He would come in on Connors's serve and hit a sliced forehand, and then come in and make Connors pass him. Or he would change the pace of the ball, which was something that he never did in the early stages of his career. He realized he needed to be a little more of a thinker on the court, which is really ironic because he was a thinker off the court. We won a few titles together as doubles partners, even though he wasn't a real good thinker tactically—he would miss volleys and forehands, so he became a much more complete player in the second part of his career.

☙❧

Nick Bollettieri has trained many of the tennis world's great champions, male and female, of recent decades at his Florida tennis academy. He never coached Ashe, but his extensive work in the sport has given him a keen eye for recognizing talent and for analyzing Ashe's potent tennis game:

Arthur's game was very methodical. He hit very flat ground strokes and had a very, very good serve. And he was very low-key—he didn't shout or rave. In fact, he was very low-key in everything that he did. Very focused. You had to beat Arthur Ashe because he wasn't going to give anything away. It was almost like playing a ghost out there. He was so unassuming and so deliberate in his mannerisms—I remember noticing how he was always putting a finger up to adjust his glasses. And he was so meticulous in his dress as well.

☙❧

Willis Thomas, Ashe's frequent teenage doubles partner, remembers how Ashe competed as much with his heart and head as he did with his (back)hands:

He was very steady and did not make many errors. He had a very natural backhand. Even when a match got very tight you couldn't get an error out of him. He rarely missed and you couldn't play with his head. He stayed in the game because he was a very good player while everyone else went on with their lives and got married or whatever. By the time the open era came, unless you were ranked, you didn't continue to play because there really wasn't any money in tennis in those days. If you were more than eighteen years old and not playing tennis in college, then you had to go and get a job.

⚮

Ashe was still an amateur and an army officer when he won his first Grand Slam event by beating **Tom Okker** *of the Netherlands to win the U.S. Open singles title in 1968. Through 2000, Ashe remained the lone African American to win the U.S. Open singles title, and Okker remembers his Open conqueror as a tennis player who didn't emphasize finesse in his game, at least not in 1968:*

I played him in the finals of the 1968 U.S. Open and had played him several times before. I always found him very difficult to play on a fast court, usually grass or a fast indoor court. He could really serve. He was always serving aces. He would also tee off on his returns all the time, so you didn't get to play too much tennis. I wasn't a power player, so I had to play kind of like a chess player when I was matched against him, and his ground strokes were very difficult to get to.

I don't think he ever was a finesse player. Not at all. Later he used more tactics and spent more time thinking about how he could change his game for different players, but he was never a finesse player. His best game was a big serve and volley, and on the return he would tee off. I remember sometimes playing doubles with him in which he would try to finesse and tried to play soft shots, and I would always be telling him, "Arthur, hit the ball hard because I know when I play you that I hate it when you hit the ball hard," but he would sometimes go back to hitting the ball soft and hitting dink shots with finesse. I think he listened to me because we got along fairly well, but he also wanted to do things his own way.

He was a good player, but there were a lot of good players. His beating Connors at Wimbledon was huge. I played junior Wimbledon starting in 1961 and was still playing Wimbledon years later as a senior, and there were very few times in there in which I stayed to watch the finals. But I watched the whole finals with Arthur against Connors because I knew it was very special. All the players were so happy when Arthur won. What I remember about that match is that Arthur hit some of his shots softer than he normally did, changing the pace, so as not to hit the ball hard all the time. Most players never thought he would win but then when he did win it was unbelievable.

I got to the Open finals in '68 by beating Tony Roche, then Pancho Gonzalez in the quarterfinals and Ken Rosewall in the semifinals. I wasn't favored against Rosewall, but I was able to beat him in four sets. It was one of my better matches. Then against Arthur, it wasn't so interesting because there was maybe one break per set and because of his being such a power player, there weren't too many rallies. It went pretty quick. I had one chance in the fifth set, I think it was, and I had it at break point but didn't make it. I didn't get too many break points the whole match.

It was nothing unusual for me to be playing him because I had played him a number of times in different places in the world. It didn't matter to me whether he was black or white or green, he was just a very good player. But the press made a big thing out of his being a black player. Then again, it was a big thing when you think about it.

⟨⟩

*Boston sportswriter and television tennis commentator **Bud Collins** recalls how Ashe's triumph at the 1968 U.S. Open was the next step in Ashe's development as a sports-world icon:*

When he won the U.S. Open, I did a series of interviews with him for the *Boston Globe*—we had something like a five-part series about what it was like being a black athlete. Early on Donald Dell sat down and asked us, "Well, what are we being paid for this?" And I said, "What do you mean 'being paid'?" And he said, "Well, this isn't like a regular interview. You're going to run a series on this." And I said, "But he's an amateur, Donald." We ended up paying Arthur some insignificant amount like $300, so I put it in my checking account until Arthur turned pro and then I gave it to him, so that was kind of funny. He turned pro after he got out of the service.

He was feeling a bit self-conscious about the deal he had that allowed him to play as an amateur because his brother, Johnnie, had served in Vietnam and been wounded. I think he served two hitches in Vietnam, and Arthur was feeling that he had a pretty cushy deal and was being paid pretty well. He got $20 a day in expense money while in New York for the 1968 U.S. Open, which was allowed, and because it was a ten-day tournament he got $200 I think it was. Arthur beat Tom Okker in the finals, but Okker got the first-place check of $14,000 as the other finalist. Actually, Open offi-

cials didn't quite know what to do with this scenario, but
they then figured that Okker was the last man standing who
could still take money, so they gave it to him.

⟡

*While Ashe was winning the U.S. Open in 1968, his father,
Arthur Sr., watched from a box seat at Forest Hills, focused
intently on his son's efforts as Arthur Jr. won the first of what
would be three Grand Slam titles. Former U.S. Davis Cup captain* **Robert Kelleher,** *now a California federal judge, sat
alongside Mr. Ashe during the entire match that day and
remembers that well, as well as the touching scene that followed:*

Mr. Ashe sat there as deeply engrossed in the outcome of
that match as any parent could ever be. He would lean one
way and then lean another way. As it was apparent toward
the end that Arthur was going to win, I said, "Mr. Ashe"—
and I always called him Mr. Ashe—"We're going to go out
and have a ceremony on the side court to present the trophy,
and I'm sure we will be giving it to Arthur, and no one would
be more pleased than I, and I'm sure everyone else here, if
you would come out and participate." He said, "Oh, that's
fine. I'd like to do that."

We set up a platform on the side court with all the
microphones and all the trimmings out there. I was out
there with Arthur and some others, and I looked up into the
area where his father and I had been sitting in this box and
spotted Mr. Ashe. He was waving his hands across his face,
as if to say, *No, no, no. I don't want to come down.* So I called
one of my assistant directors over and told him to try to talk
Mr. Ashe into coming down and he did. Mr. Ashe came out

on the platform and we had the usual kind of stuff in presenting the trophies and so forth. After I handed the winner's trophy to Arthur, he looked over toward his father who had tears on his face, and Arthur reached across and put his arm across his father's shoulders, and, by golly, tears came down Arthur's face, too. That was probably the most meaningful occurrence I have ever been involved in with tennis. It was a heart-wrenching thing. It was such a beautiful scene of father and son. I have that picture somewhere and I run across it every now and then, and it puts a lump in my throat.

⚭

One striking characteristic of men's tennis during Ashe's active years as a player was how players took the time to get to know each other off the court without the distraction of entourages shielding them from the other players, as **Okker** *points out:*

There weren't as many tennis players back then, and we only had one tournament a week, where now you might have two or three in a week all around the world. For the good players, it was a pretty small group in which everyone knew each other pretty well, and we went to the same places from one week to the next, so it was a much closer friendship than the players today have. No one traveled with coaches and you pretty much saw the same guys every week, and some became pretty good friends. Also, there wasn't as much a sense of nationalism then even though we had players competing against each other from all over the world. The only events that were based on international ties were Davis Cup matches, and those involved only a few weeks out of the year, so most of the time you were playing only for yourself and not necessarily for your country.

⌒⠶⠶⠶⠤

Kelleher was Ashe's first Davis Cup captain, in 1963, and already was quite familiar with the native Virginian's games dating back a few years:

I remember Arthur when he first turned up at UCLA and was still a teenager. He never changed very much over the years. Oh, he matured during that period when he was in his twenties, but he was still essentially the same gentle yet tough competitor of a guy. He always treated me as his senior and always addressed me as Captain. He confessed to me early on that his father had been his biggest influence in his life. Mr. Ashe was a stern taskmaster and monitored Arthur's actions very closely on and off the tennis court. He continued throughout his life to be a strong influence on Arthur.

⌒⠶⠶⠶⠤

Davis Cup play played a big role in defining Ashe's career, both as a player and as a U.S. team captain. **Donald Dell,** *Ashe's long-time lawyer, manager, friend, and confidant—himself a former Davis Cup player and captain—offers snippets of his early history with Ashe as well as tidbits of his experience involving the Davis Cup:*

I went to Yale as an undergraduate and Virginia Law School. I played the circuit for a number of years in and out of law school and played the Davis Cup five times. I was on one of the teams that was captained by Bob Kelleher, a federal judge now, and this was in '63 and '64. Then he became the President of the USTA in '67 and '68, and he appointed me captain when I was twenty-nine years old. I was working for Sargent Shriver at the time, who was running the Office of Economic Opportunity and the Peace Corps, and by happenstance I was also heavily involved in Bobby Kennedy's campaign for the presidency. I was organizing five states as the lead advance. I would have two or three guys working in each state for me as advance men. When Bobby was killed in June of 1968, I had already accepted the job as Davis Cup captain in March of 1968, so now I was in the midst of doing the campaign at that time when we weren't doing the Davis Cup campaign. Arthur and Stan were with Bobby the day before he died. They were running up and down the state of California on the back end of the train with Senator Kennedy. Then we flew to Charlotte on a Sunday to get ready to play Ecuador in the Davis Cup two weeks later, and Bobby was killed on Tuesday at the Ambassador Hotel after winning the California primary.

I have a long background in tennis. Arthur Ashe and Stan Smith were the two biggest players on our team in 1968 and 1969. We had lost the Davis Cup for five years in a row to various teams like Ecuador and Mexico, but I made it a big issue for the team that we would have a mission. We never lost in '68 or '69, and I may be one of the only captains who never lost. I had also been the youngest captain ever. I spent an awful lot of time with Arthur during those two years because I wasn't married and the politics had been demolished by Kennedy's death. I was traveling around with the team almost full-time. I still had a job in Washington, D.C., but working on the Davis Cup was taking up the bulk of my time.

Ashe had a flair for fashion that matched his flair on the court. (Jim Osborne, AP/Wide World Photos)

As great a tennis champion as he was, Ashe once admitted that his mind would sometimes wander during tennis matches:

I'll start thinking about anything but the match—girls, a horse race. I don't know. At Sydney this past year, I was playing John Newcombe in the finals. I won the first set. Then all of a sudden I started thinking about this stewardess, Bella, I had met. *Oh-h-h-h.* She was Miss Trinidad of 1962. I just kept seeing her—this gorgeous face, this beautiful creature—and the next thing I know the match is over and Newcombe's won. And here's how crazy I am, too. I never even took Bella out. I was too scared. I figured she was just too beautiful for me.[1]

∫

Dennis Ralston was another of Ashe's tennis brethren whose association with Ashe dated back to the sixties. It's an association that also had roots in Davis Cup play. Ralston, who would later coach Chris Evert and Roscoe Tanner among others, won the U.S. Open singles twice and the French Open once. He also had ample involvement with the Davis Cup experience, both as a captain and player:

I knew Arthur through his transition. I turned pro in '66 and he remained an amateur, and I got involved with Arthur again in '68 and '69 when I was the Davis Cup coach and we played a lot of doubles together. I traveled with the team and became pretty close friends with Arthur. He won the '68 U.S. Open, but I still felt that all the established pros, guys like Laver, were stronger. But Arthur really improved in the early seventies.

Arthur and I would beat the heck out of (Stan) Smith and (Bob) Lutz almost every time we played them in Davis Cup practices. We were a pretty good team. We won the South American one year and lost in the finals at Wimbledon one year, 6-4, in the fifth set to Laver and

Emerson, and that's one that we should have won. We had a disagreement on the court during that match when Arthur started telling me to get my first serve in, and I said to him, "What do you think I'm trying to do?" We were up, 4-2, in the fourth set and ahead two sets to one when he threw that comment out to me. Arthur sometimes just said what he thought.

I remember the first time that he played a match that was live and that really counted—it was a doubles match with me down in Mexico, and he was so nervous that he almost turned white, really. That's how nervous he was for the first two and a half sets and finally he started to play well. But until then it had been like I was playing on my own against three guys for almost three sets. Then he played well and we won in four sets. He played well against Mexico, but that was on his service.

Playing in Dallas for another Davis Cup match was a big deal. We were supposed to play at the Dallas Country Club, but they said we couldn't play there; I didn't find out until much later that the reason we played somewhere else was because Arthur was black. Still, Davis Cup play to him was very important because he represented the United States as a player and later as a captain. Arthur had this reputation of being Mr. Cool, but like anyone else he had a full range of emotions and had just learned how to be able to keep them under control.

As for Davis Cup play itself, in those days there weren't any personal coaches, so I was the coach for all of them and we worked on things that I had learned from guys like Pancho Gonzalez, and knowing that all of the Australians were always in great shape, that was always one of the things we worked on, being in great shape. I would have them do a lot of running and drills for quickness, stuff like that. Their games were established and I didn't tinker with those much.

❧

Kelleher offers this assessment of Ashe's tennis game:

I always had the highest regard for Arthur as a person and as a player. I was never surprised when he won because he was capable and at his best he could beat anybody and everybody. He was an aggressive serve-and-volley player. He had a great serve and a great net game. By the time he played Connors, you could say he was a shrewd player, because the way he beat Connors was a surprise to everybody: He exploited what few weaknesses Connors had. He served wide to Jimmy's forehand because his forehand wasn't as good as a backhand.

Arthur had some very close advisers, such as Dennis Ralston and Donald Dell. They polished up his game. It wasn't so much that he had many rough edges on it, he just needed to learn when to attack and when to defend, and he had to learn a little better how to use the great skills that he had.

❧

Kelleher gives some added perspective on Davis Cup play and how Ashe fit into that picture early on:

A captain picks a team to win the Cup. The picks you make depend on who you're going to play, what time of year it is and who's available. In 1962 we were playing against Venezuela and I think it was in Denver, Colorado, and Arthur was good enough to play and he won. But we lost to

Mexico that year, and I did not take Arthur to Mexico because I didn't think he was good enough—there were two singles players at the time better than he was. The following year, he became one of the top five ranked players. By the time we were ready to take off to go around the world and play Great Britain, India, and Australia, Ralston and Billy McKinley were clearly the players who were going to win the Cup for us. I had a very frank conversation with Arthur before we took off to go to England. I said, "I'm not going to take you, Arthur, because you're not going to play. I'm going to go with Ralston and McKinley, and I don't think it's in your interests at your stage of the game, having your problems"—which was an acknowledgment that as a black, he might encounter difficulties in India or anywhere he went. He was very understanding, although I was later told by someone that he was heartbroken that he was not selected to make that trip. But he accepted it.

It took him another five years to come into his own, to include winning the Open in 1968. That was his first really big win. He had kind of up and down periods during that time as he was sharpening his game. Then it was another seven years before he won Wimbledon, so I think he was still in the process of growing up.

❧

*Tennis and golf are alike in that they are sports in which individuals are sometimes called to act on the honor system, as **Stan Smith** recalls from one of his many memorable matches also involving Ashe:*

One match of particular significance was the final of the

WCT Tour in 1973, and this was an event that was probably at the level of the Grand Slam events at the time. The WCT Tour had almost all of the top players, and this particular year all of the top players were there, players such as Rod Laver, Ken Rosewall, and John Newcombe, and Arthur and I happened to play each other in the finals. This was in Dallas, where two things happened to us that were kind of interesting. By this time, we were very close friends; we had been on the overseas tours and played Davis Cup together, and we had known each other five or six years.

We had played each other a number of times, so playing against each other was nothing new for us. Most people assume that in the finals of a tournament, all of the other players who are there and have already been eliminated have stayed behind to watch the finals, but in reality all players are gone by then, because once players are out of the tournament, they're gone. That means there's usually nobody left behind for the finalists to practice with. So Arthur and I ended up practicing with each other out on the center court, which really was the only court available that had the kind of surface we would be playing on in the next day's finals. People walking by would ask us, "Why are you practicing with each other?" We would tell them, one, because there's nobody else to practice with, and, second, we know each other's game so well that it really doesn't matter. There's nothing about any aspect of our respective games that the other did not know well.

The second memorable thing about this Dallas WCT match was that near the end of the match, in the fourth set, Arthur was at the net where he hit a ball, a short ball. I was running forward, got my racket on it, and got it over his head as a lob, and then he hit it back, and I hit an overhead. If I remember right, it was one of the biggest points of the match. I think it might have been a break point because I served out the match in the next game. That lob was very controversial because Arthur didn't know whether or not I had gotten the ball before it bounced a second time. The umpire said he thought I got it, but people were shouting and people really getting into it because it was the fourth set of a very close match. It was good tennis. After some indecision from the officials, Arthur finally looked over at me and said, "Did you get to it?" And I said, "I thought I got it." And he said, "Hey, if he thinks he got it, he got it." That demonstrated his faith in me as a friend and my being honest.

⌒⋙⋘⌒

Ashe's greatest tennis victory had to be his upset of Jimmy Connors in the singles at Wimbledon in 1975. **Collins** *remembers it well:*

That was just wonderful. Connors at that time was regarded as invincible. He was the defending champion at Wimbledon and defending champion at the U.S. Open, and he had just had a phenomenal record the year before. Everybody liked Arthur, but he was like a 10-1 underdog. I remember (newspaper reporter) Mike Lupica and I both being worried that Arthur was going to be embarrassed. I think everybody was worried about that and we even worried about Arthur being there because of the way that Connors had beaten up on (Ken) Rosewall the year before. We all felt the same thing would happen to Arthur. Connors had just looked so invulnerable in the tournament, and of course, there was no love lost between the two because, for one

A beaming Ashe holds the Wimbledon men's singles trophy aloft moments after upsetting Jimmy Connors in 1975. (AP/Wide World Photos)

thing, Connors was suing Arthur (for libel) at the time. Arthur came out in his U.S.A. jacket, and this was when Connors had refused to play in Davis Cup. It was masterly the way Arthur went about it, and then it almost seemed so effortless in how he went about winning the first set.

Arthur had the perfect game plan, just to slice the ball to Connors's backhand and then just get out there and bunt the volley. Connors was confused. But even then, after Arthur had won the first set, I still thought Connors was just too much and that, Hey, it would be okay to lose in four sets. It was that kind of negative defensive thinking that I'm sure most people had except for perhaps Arthur, Donald Dell, and Dennis Ralston. Then Arthur won the next set and suddenly it was, "Gosh, he might win." Then he lost the third and you knew that Connors was such a great fighter, but then it worked out all right for Arthur.

I remember interviewing him afterwards, and we both had smiles as wide as the Mississippi River. It was marvelous, a great accomplishment. Of all the Wimbledon finals I've ever covered, that was probably the second most warmly received. The first would be Virginia Wade winning in 1977, when everybody sang to her. With Arthur there was such warmth, and nobody liked Connors. Jimmy has grown on people since, but then he was the bad boy and very truculent. And Arthur was such a long shot and everyone knew he was such a gentleman who had served his country and had done everything right, and everyone realized how unusual it would be for a black to win at Wimbledon. It was historic and it was pleasing. I was hit later by it when I came home to Boston and went through customs, where most of the places were manned by Irish people, who were not overly fond of blacks. And when I went through customs the guy said to me, "Wasn't it wonderful what Ashe did?" and that really affected me.

❧

Thomas knew Ashe's game well enough to know that what many observers of the 1975 Wimbledon singles final between Ashe and Connors figured to be a master stroke of strategical genius on Ashe's part was actually something old that Ashe had perfected many years earlier:

I was talking to him one time about playing on grass. We got around to talking about how Arthur had come up with this particular shot of hitting it low and short to Connors's forehand, which was Jimmy's weakness. We were laughing about it because people were talking after the match how Arthur had developed this shot just for Connors, when actually that's how we used to hit our forehands when we were kids. He laughed and said, "Yeah, they thought I had developed something special when all it was was a shot we had used all the time as kids." There was nothing secret about it. Today I call it the "ghetto chop" because all of the black kids use it, putting underspin on the forehand. You just don't see a lot of people using it. We got a good kick out of that.

❧

Dell also recalls Wimbledon in 1975 as a special moment:

It was a very intense, emotional time because Connors was suing the ATP for $40 million saying that he had been excluded from the French Open, and Arthur was the president of the ATP, and here he is playing Connors in the finals.

Arthur went out and beat Connors in four sets. Generally, Arthur did not play well against Connors because Connors was left-handed and Arthur didn't like playing against left-handers. He didn't like returning serves against lefthanders, particularly Laver. Laver dominated Arthur, winning the first seventeen times they played against each other.

In that particular match against Jimmy at Wimbledon, Arthur had a strategy on how to play Jimmy. Ironically, I ended up representing Connors later on for about eight years, so I knew both of them quite well. On about the third changeover during the match, Arthur pulled out a piece of paper from his racket cover, and on it were three or four points that we had gone over the night before. Basic things like, "Get your first serve in," and "When you come into the net, watch his passing shot," and "His backhand is much more effective than his forehand." "Keep the ball low to his forehand side," because Connors had a weak forehand, particularly on the approach shot if the ball was kept low. If you go back and look at tape of the match, you see Arthur after the third game pull out this piece of paper, and after he started reading it people thought he was meditating or something. He was sitting in his chair and was really studying his notes based on what we had strategized the night before.

That was an exciting time, and right after he won the match—and you can see it from the tape of the match—he immediately twirled with a very uplifted fist. My wife (Carol) and I were sitting in the front row of the player box, sort of overhanging the court, and he was actually waving to us a fist of joy, only for several papers to say it was the black power salute, or the Black Panthers' salute. But that had nothing to do with that, although he still had to repudiate that.

Pam Shriver didn't become a professional tennis player until the late seventies, but she was a big fan of the sport from an early age and remembers the 1975 Wimbledon singles final as a watershed moment in Ashe's career:

A lot of times tennis players are defined by the matches in which they played, and the finals of Wimbledon in 1975 when he beat Connors in a big upset will always define Arthur as far as his tennis playing goes. I was thirteen at the time and I can remember just how calm he was throughout that final match with Connors and how incredibly focused he was. Even as young as I was, I was able to get a good sense of the significance of his victory and how he was playing exactly the kind of game that Jimmy just couldn't handle. It was really something to see.

✎✎✎

*Another of **Shriver**'s Wimbledon memories involving Ashe came several years later, when Ashe unwittingly cost his future TV commentating cohort a cherished shot at playing on center court:*

I can remember my first Wimbledon in part because of the unwitting role Arthur played in denying me a chance that year to play on the center court. I was due out on the court one day for a doubles match, which was to be the last match on center court for the day, while Arthur was in the next-to-last match playing doubles with Yannick Noah, an up and comer out of Cameroon that Arthur had "discovered" and who was only something like seventeen years old at the time. We were waiting to go onto the court when they went into a fifth set, and that was when they played three out of five in doubles, which they don't do anymore. The match ended up going to 15-13 for the last set, so our match ended up getting moved to an outside court.

ᕰᕮᕮ

DD Eisenberg *covered tennis beginning in the seventies for the now-defunct* Philadelphia Bulletin. *In getting to know Ashe and his contemporaries, she acquired an interesting perspective of tennis in those days:*

In the sixties and seventies these were all college-educated guys. A little later we started getting players who had gone to college maybe one year before turning pro and they hadn't had as many years of life. Those guys who had been playing in the sixties had traveled around the world playing Davis Cup matches and had been through traumatic events like the Vietnam War and the deaths of Bobby Kennedy and Martin Luther King Jr. It seems like they had a lot more to talk about because of those influences mixed with their education. Then you had players coming up in the seventies such as Chris Evert and Rosie Casals, who had been playing tennis and doing little else since they were kids. Many of these players never had the chance to go to college because they turned pro so early. This was a very special time because these guys had other interests, read books, and could give you quotes in paragraphs.

I can remember also covering hockey with the Philadelphia Flyers, who had guys like Bobby Clarke and Dave "the Hammer" Schultz. There was such a difference between trying to interview those athletes, who couldn't put a paragraph together, let alone a sentence, assuming they had their teeth in, and guys like Smith, Lutz, and Ashe who were very well educated and very well-trained athletes. They had good times and the occasional beer, but I never saw them losing it because they had too much to lose. It was a great beat. There were also issues such as Martina Navratilova's defecting to the United States from Czechoslovakia, (transsexual) Renee Richards, and all these other international issues that you were covering. Arthur even by himself was going through so many things such as when he went to South Africa and writing his books about African-American athletes, that there just seemed to be so much to write about. In those days, there was also the understanding that you didn't delve as much into their personal lives. If you knew about something personal and sensitive, you still wouldn't write about it. There weren't many women covering sports then and that's another thing about Arthur, he was very tolerant of us and he took us seriously. We were serious reporters just trying to cover the beat. We had a lot on our shoulders in those days. Arthur was very well-read, and he always had something different and fresh to say every day.

⚭

In writing an epitaph piece for Sports Illustrated *following Ashe's death on February 6, 1993,* **Kenny Moore** *offered this succinct evaluation of Ashe's on-court performance:*

Ashe was the best at leaving every shot behind. He played each stroke as if it were for life and death and then instantly abstained from regret or celebration because there was another shot to play. It was inefficient, even self-destructive to waste energy raging at himself or his opponent or the umpire, even though to do so is wholly human. Too, he learned early that his unnatural cool was often so unsettling that it could be a tactical weapon."[2]

❧

Eliot Teltscher joined the tennis circuit just as Ashe's career was winding down, although Teltscher came along in time to get a good taste of what it was like to play against Ashe:

Arthur had a great serve, although it was not like the big booming serves of 130 miles per hour that you see today. He was extremely good at placing it and really good at mixing it up. And he had a great wide serve, as well as a great backhand. I also thought he moved the ball around the court quite well. Arthur played with a lot of touch and a lot of feel. But he played a game that was sort of different from anyone else's I was familiar with. It was different from the standpoint that it certainly wouldn't fit into today's game. I thought he played more like the way McEnroe played in that he had a lot of touch and a lot of feel, too. Arthur was very creative. When I first played him, it turned out to be a type of game that was a little bit out of the norm, and I wasn't used to it. It was tough breaking his serve, and on top of that he would come in on you a lot and put a good amount of pressure on you.

When you play a guy ten times, you probably start to get a feeling for his personality. I never really was able to develop a feel for Arthur's personality from playing him, although by the time I started playing him he was already a legend, having won Wimbledon, the U.S. Open, and some other big tournaments. When I played him the first time, I was pretty intimidated and it wasn't because of anything that he did that day. But that's part of it. He had a difficult game to play, especially for me.

༄༅

Harry Marmion, past president of the United States Tennis Association, joined the USTA in the mid-seventies, giving him a ringside seat at Davis Cup play, to include Ashe's five-year stint, starting in 1980, as U.S. Davis Cup captain:

I got involved in the USTA in the mid-seventies, then I got on the board of the USTA. Worked my way up to get on the board and got on the board in 1988.

I was an academic, a college president, and he liked to talk about things like that. He was a very intellectual guy. The first time I met Arthur was at a Davis Cup match in Ireland. He was captain of the U.S. Davis Cup team at the time, and we were there to play a match against the Republic of Ireland. It was quite unusual for us to be playing in Ireland. John McEnroe was playing for the United States that year, and the Irish fans in Ireland liked him. The team there also included Eliot Teltscher and McEnroe's doubles partner, Peter Fleming.

We were out at the hotel where the team was staying when I met Arthur, and I started to talk to him and found him to be very nice. He did get himself into some difficulty with the establishment of the USTA because it was perceived that he didn't have much control over the U.S. players. They didn't necessarily dress properly or act properly, so there was a concern about his lack of leadership in terms of leading the fellows on the team. For one thing, McEnroe wouldn't practice with the team and he wouldn't travel with the team, and it was very difficult for Arthur. He was a very retiring individual. It's a lot of responsibility and we've had very, very fine captains of our Davis Cup teams. Arthur was a good Davis Cup captain, but he just didn't quite have that mindset of leadership you would prefer. He was just kind of a quiet, retiring guy.

In my opinion, and I stress *opinion*, being the captain of the U.S. team, in general, involves a diplomatic role, one where you've got to interact with other countries, which is particularly important for the United States because we're always being looked down on, or looked up at—however you want to put it—by people who want to see how we're going to react if we lose a match or whatever. You're always "on." It's not a matter of just playing tennis, which is something that's hard to understand when you live in the United States. You have to be very careful when you're traveling abroad. You have to be very forward looking about how you carry the flag or how you look when flying in or flying out, where you go, how you dress. And it's up to the captain to set the style.

Another thing you like to see in any Davis Cup captain is the ability to be a good public relations vehicle for the nation. Don't ever be snotty with the press. Always be looking forward. Be diligent about how you select the team. Be informed. Know everything you can about the players you'll be playing against, and know a little about the countries you'll be playing against. Basically, it's an ambassador's job and it involves very little coaching with the players, who are probably making a little more money than you are. As John McEnroe now says [until McEnroe resigned as U.S. Davis Cup captain in November 2000], it's hard to know how to motivate players when you only get them for four weeks out of the year. When you stop to think about it, maybe now John has a better idea of what Arthur went through twenty years ago when John was playing on the Davis Cup team. What goes around comes around.

☙❧

Teltscher, now a USTA regional coach for southern California, adds his perspectives on playing for Ashe in Davis Cup competition:

I played Arthur a couple of times that I remember. I remember losing to him at a tournament in Columbus, Ohio, my first year on tour, and losing to him in a tournament in Richmond, Virginia. I know I played him more than that, but it's hard to remember all the matches.

My involvement with him was more with the Davis Cup, when he was captain and I was one of the American players. This was at a time when John McEnroe was playing, too, and he and John obviously had different views. There was a little bit of controversy during that time. Generally, you're more in a cheerleader role as Davis Cup captain because you're talking about something that involves only four weeks out of the year, so there's a limit in how much influence you're going to have in that time. Maybe cheerleader is an unfair term, so perhaps it involves something more in the middle between coordinating and coaching the team, and the other part is motivational. I played in maybe half of the matches. I never sat down with Arthur and had a long conversation with him on his views on life or anything like that. I wasn't that close to him. And I didn't keep in touch with him on the weeks I didn't play. Age difference was part of it, and, besides, Arthur wasn't traveling much anymore except for the Davis Cup matches. Whatever memories I do have of him at that time was of the battles between him and John to tell you the truth. Arthur was a fairly quiet guy, or at least it seemed to me.

One way to gauge how popular Davis Cup play is by comparing it to golf's Ryder Cup. I can remember the Ryder Cup being on at something like five in the morning when they were playing in Europe, and I don't even really care about golf, but I loved watching it. However, if they had those matches going on four times a year, like what happens with the Davis Cup, I don't think there would be as much interest in the Ryder Cup. How much interest would there be in the Olympics if they were held four times a year, instead of once every four years? In that regard, the Davis Cup loses a little something. In the Ryder Cup, having it every other year adds a little luster to it. My Davis Cup experience is more exciting to me now than it was at the time, although it was exciting to be part of a Davis Cup winning team. It's never been that big of a deal in this country as it is in other countries. The Davis Cup has recently gotten more publicity in the last year because of John's being captain, and I don't remember our making any of the front pages of big newspapers when we won.

We were a different kind of player. Arthur was somebody who liked to go to the net, and he wanted me more and more at the net. But I didn't really want to be there. Because this involved only a few weeks out of the year, I didn't think it best if I were to change my game just for the matches. I kind of played the way I thought was best for me. Maybe he thought there was a chance for me to improve and be a better player if I committed more and then I would move up (in the rankings), and maybe he was right. I don't know. I decided I'd better stay back more.

One match I remember in particular was when we were playing Germany. We were down, 2-1, in the matches and if I were to beat my opponent in a singles match, it would make it 2-all, setting us up for a win by giving Aaron Krickstein a chance to clinch a victory against Boris Becker. Well, I was down two sets to one and I got involved in a pretty big argument at that point in the match because I thought I had gotten a bad call. As it turned out, I ended up winning the match. Arthur and I had a kind of a mixed thing about that argument I had because my personality actually was closer to McEnroe's than it was to Arthur's. Simply, his view of it was a little different. That was just not the way he was brought up to handle things. I got very emotional about it. My opponent hit a ball that I thought was out, and it was called in. Arthur tried to be supportive of me, but he just didn't agree because that's not how he wanted to handle things. He didn't intervene so much as to just try and keep me from arguing. There were times I felt he could be a little more supportive and argue for us a little more, when he was probably thinking, "Why don't you just shut up and play?" I thought it was a match that I should win, and it was a match to keep us alive.

All of the Davis Cup matches by themselves are so important. It's not like a regular tournament where you can sort of work your way into it. That's why (Jim) Courier has done so well over the years—he could always get himself up even when his game was falling apart in one match. The Davis Cup is a different thing—I felt more pressure playing Davis Cup than anything else I've ever played. Arthur didn't really give me a pep talk before that match I had against the German player, but I didn't really want him to either. I mean, it wasn't like this was my first year on tour and I had never been involved in something of this magnitude before. I kind of knew what I had to do. I just needed to be able to relax and play, because no matter what, things will turn out the way things will turn out. Period. It wasn't Arthur's way to come up and try to give me a pep talk: I would have been stunned. That just isn't his personality, and whenever anyone steps outside his or her personality they end up looking a little foolish. It wouldn't have been good if he had done that.

⚬⟋⟍⚬

During his reign as U.S. Davis Cup captain, Ashe led the Americans to a 13-3 record that included back-to-back overall triumphs in 1981 and 1982. Still, there was some criticism directed at Ashe because of what some felt should have been an even better record, especially with the likes of Connors and McEnroe on the team. Ashe himself had to wonder if he led his teams as well as he could have:

To be more effective, I suppose, I should have been more gregarious at times, and at other times more aggressive. I should have tried harder to impose my will on the players. But I couldn't do that, and I have to live with the consequences. I accepted the fact that as much as I want to lead others, and love to be around other people, in some essential way I am something of a loner.[3]

⚬⟋⟍⚬

*One of the tennis players Ashe mentored off and on over the years was **Rodney Harmon,** also an African-American native of Richmond, whose best shot at stardom came when he made it to the quarterfinals of the U.S. Open in 1982. Ashe was never Harmon's personal coach, but he was squirming in his seat at Forest Hills for the entire match as Harmon took on Connors:*

One year, 1982, I was fortunate enough to get to the quarterfinals of the U.S. Open. I remember playing in the round of sixteen and my opponent was Eliot Teltscher. I was still in college at the time and Arthur was telling me to not get my hopes up too high. Arthur sat with Willis Smith (Ashe's tennis cohort from his early days and later Harmon's coach) for the two sets and we split the sets, then, when I was behind in the third set, he left, although I came back and won it. Then Arthur came back and I lost the fourth set. So he left again and then I won the match. He didn't see me win the last two sets I won, which was kind of interesting.

After a day off, I was then scheduled to play Jimmy Connors in a quarterfinal. In the locker room before that match with Connors, Arthur came to me and said that I should play him using a particular style, which was basically the same strategy he had used when he had beaten Connors in the finals of 1975. So I tried it when I first went out, even though that wasn't how I had played to make it that far. I ended up abandoning that approach and went back to playing the way that had gotten me there. Connors ended up beating me in three sets and some people came up to me afterward and said, "You know, you should have played your own game and not used that other strategy." The thing is, Arthur was trying to help me, and the other thing he thought is that it would give me a better opportunity to win.

He had told me to go to Connors's forehand and hit the ball offspeed a lot, and don't serve and volley a lot because it will give him too much of a target, where I had been winning by serve and volley and hitting a lot of topspin and attacking a lot. In hindsight, my chance to beat him that day was probably minimal if any. My best shot probably would have been if I could have employed the strategy that Arthur gave me to the best of my ability, but I just couldn't get it done. Some people heard about it and that involved a lack of maturity on my part because I should have kept my mouth shut. People were asking me why I didn't play my own game, but what was I, maybe nineteen years old at the time? So I gave it a try, even though people later were saying "Why didn't you do this?" or "Why didn't you do that?" But the key thing is that without Arthur's help through the years, I wouldn't have been there in the first place.

⌘

Thomas was Harmon's coach in those days, but found himself being joined by Ashe and others surrounding Harmon moments before that 1982 Open quarterfinal against Connors:

Arthur and I had a couple of run-ins over the years. One of them was when Rodney was in the quarterfinals of the Open and he was playing against Connors, after having just beaten Eliot Teltscher. One thing you've got to know about me is that I've always wanted to be kind of a laid-back person behind the scenes, not out in the forefront. So of course everybody wanted to cut in and say they had been coaching Rodney when in fact I had been coaching him since he was a kid. He had been to Bollettieri's camp, he had been to

SMU (under Ralston) and he had been helped along the way by Arthur, and then you had the Davis Cup coaches coaching him. Anyway, Rodney just kind of worked his way through the draw and all of a sudden he beats Teltscher in the round of sixteen to get into the quarterfinals. Then he had to play Connors the next day.

Well, Rodney and I always had this little ritual before the matches in which we would go out to a nearby park just to get away from all that was going on, and do this about twenty minutes before a match so we could quietly talk about things. But now all of a sudden here it is the quarterfinals of the U.S. Open and now you have all this pageantry. So they expect you to be around before your match earlier so everyone can look at you and all that sort of stuff. So this time we go out to the park earlier than usual and walk around talking some, joking and trying to relax. So when it's twenty minutes to eleven with his match scheduled for eleven, we go back in and I leave Rodney, telling him I just need to take a couple of minutes to run over to the box office and pick up a couple of tickets for some folks. I tell him, "Now, Rodney, just go straight to the locker room and go upstairs, go into a bathroom, slip into a toilet stall, and shut the door, and no one is going to bother you. Just sit there until it's time to go out to the court."

Well, by the time I get back, there's Bollettieri, Ashe, everybody, but Rodney. He was surrounded by everybody and there's Arthur writing some notes for playing against Connors for him to take out on the court and glance at during the match. I am mad as hell by the time I get there. I am seething. So Rodney goes out and didn't play well at all. He wasn't playing his normal game. Afterward on our way to the press conference, I said to him, "Now, Rodney, you've got to be honest about what happened. But don't go so far as to talk about Arthur." One thing we never did as black folks was to talk about each other in front of the press, and that's something I always told Rodney. "Don't air it in the press." Anyway, Rodney was asked a series of questions about his not playing like he normally played. Later on, Arthur apologized to me, saying he was sorry he had said anything to confuse Rodney. About a month or two after that Arthur got a number of us black coaches together and brought us all up to New York and had a meeting in his apartment, where he said he was going to help us. I think it was at that point that Arthur sort of came back to us to help give back more to blacks in tennis. He really loosened up.

⁊ᴍᴍꝯ

Harmon *followed Ashe's career closely enough to have some interesting insights into what made Ashe one of the sport's best players ever—except when it came to one particular rival:*

He lost so many close matches to Rod Laver. He had a lot of matches in which he came so close to winning but couldn't quite pull it out. But he always persevered. He always stayed so composed out there, when there were other guys out there acting like such a fool.

⁊ᴍᴍꝯ

Ralston *also weighs in with a summation of Ashe, the tennis player:*

It was fun coaching Arthur. He worked hard and had his own style; it was slash. He had a great backhand and a great serve, and a dangerous forehand but could hit the fence with it, too. He wasn't that great at the net, but he worked at it and got better because he was smart and wanted to get better.

3

BLACK AND WHITE

The easy way out in describing what Arthur Ashe did as the first African-American male to hit it big in tennis is to compare it to what Jackie Robinson had done in baseball almost fifty years before. But as much a pioneer as he was, and as courageous as he was in breaking baseball's color line, Robinson had a certain advantage over Ashe: Black baseball players already had access to a caliber of play practically equal to the major leagues—the Negro Leagues. Hundreds of thousands of black youths already had access to areas where they could easily play a pickup baseball game, where access to tennis courts was more limited to facilities such as whites-only country clubs and off-limits public courts.

Ashe went against the grain as a young African American growing up in the forties and fifties. He encountered well-established prejudice and accessibility blockades, yet found a way to develop his tennis skills well enough to become a world champion. Ashe was born into a segregated world in Richmond, where monuments paid homage to Confederate generals. But Ashe himself, through his words and deeds, had a lot to do with bridging that gap, at least in Richmond. Upon his death at age forty-nine in 1993, Ashe became not just the first African American but the first person, period, since Confederate general Stonewall Jackson, to lie in state in the Virginia governor's mansion.

Ashe's tennis career was loaded with firsts, most of which were tied to the fact that he was black: first African American to win the NCAA singles title; winner of the first U.S. Open men's singles title; first African American to win men's singles at Wimbledon; etc., etc. But Ashe did more than win in becoming a great champion; he used tennis and his accomplishments in the sport as a platform to become a shaker and mover listened to by leaders across cultures and national boundaries. And he was his own man in doing so. Ashe didn't cater to the directives of black activists such as Jesse Jackson. Instead, he carefully considered the pros and cons of all issues before deciding what his course of action or beliefs would be. He was a voracious reader and an accomplished writer, and he spoke and wrote as his own conscience directed him. In that regard, Ashe truly was a liberated man.

If there was a watershed moment in Ashe's life as a self-directed black activist, it was in 1973 when he finally was granted a visa to visit racially divided South Africa to play in the South African Open. Ashe didn't go to South Africa just to play in a tennis tournament, however; he was there to raise worldwide awareness of apartheid. It might have been his boldest stroke ever.

Ashe often walked a tightrope between black and white during his lifetime, sometimes thought of as too much of a black activist by one side and too much of an Uncle Tom by the other. Ashe never could please everyone, and he probably realized better than anyone he needn't even try. As long-time sports journalist and Ashe confidant **Frank Deford** *points out, Ashe may have been the epitome of someone who truly was his own man, liberated in his secure awareness of who he was and what he stood for:*

As the first (prominent) black male tennis player, Arthur was the only black in a sea of white faces. It was hard in other ways, too, in that there were well-intentioned black people who wanted to take care of him. So he'd go to a tournament in some place and right away black people would descend upon him—black strangers. And there was the pressure of being polite to them, but he really didn't want to hang out with a lot of strangers. He had so many friends on the tour. He always had to straddle that line, and anytime he would make a mistake people would jump on him and say he was an Uncle Tom. He couldn't win. The first time (prominent African-American sports sociologist) Harry Edwards went to see Arthur was in 1968, and that was when he tried to get Arthur to boycott and all that kind of thing. I think Harry's first reaction on meeting Arthur was that, Gosh, Ashe is a Tom. It was only later that he understood that Arthur had to do things his way, and his way was right for Arthur Ashe.

The thing with Arthur was that he refused to just go along with the flow. He always made his own decisions, and some of those decisions were very, very hard. He had to make decisions related to tennis, too, because he was one of the political leaders. Boycott Wimbledon and all the traditions that tennis had? He somehow managed to do all the things that he believed in, and was able to do them in such a way that he rarely made enemies. It was amazing. I think people just realized how forthright and honest he was, and how decent he was. It was hard to get mad at Arthur Ashe.

❧

*Another journalist who was keenly aware of Ashe's unique identity as an African American in a "white man's sport" was **Bud Collins,** whose memories of Ashe date far enough back to when blacks were still commonly referred to as "Negroes." Race was an issue when Collins first met Ashe, although over time Collins came to understand just how deeply independent and fair-minded Ashe was:*

The first memory I have of him is in the mid-1960s, when he came to Boston to play in the U.S Doubles Championship at Longwood Cricket Club, and of course he was an oddity because he was the only black player in the field. On top of that he was not talkative. I didn't really get to know him until later, so at the time I didn't know if he was shy or if he was being cautious, or simply whether he was wary of reporters. Interestingly enough, I talked to a lot of people who were his friends, or at least they seemed to be his friends, people who were from southern California and were also college age. This was when Arthur was still at UCLA. They didn't want to talk about him much and I think it's because they respected his wish for privacy. So there wasn't much of a story except his being black, and back then we said Negro. So it wasn't really until he played Davis Cup and won a couple of matches against Mexico in Dallas that he seemed to start opening up a little bit. I remember him saying, "I wish you wouldn't keep referring to me as the Negro tennis player. You don't refer to Willie Mays as the Negro center fielder." That made sense, but on the other hand he was singular in the sport of tennis.

In 1967 he played Davis Cup and again against Mexico in Mexico City and that was at a time when there was so much awareness of what was going on with the Black Panthers and some other things going on that were troublesome. About this time I remember talking to Arthur for a column I was writing and he said, "I'm not a brick thrower. I think there are other ways to go about this." Then in 1968, the great break for both of us came when he returned to Boston. This was the first year of open tennis, and Arthur was still an amateur then. The USTA was worried about open tennis, afraid that it would flop. They wanted to continue what had been always U.S. championships and they put it in Boston. It was called the U.S. Amateur Championships and he won that for his first important title, beating Bob Lutz in five sets. That was also the first year of PBS having a nationwide telecast of tennis. I was doing it alone (TV commentating) in those days. After he won, he came up and gave me all the time in the world, and I ended up interviewing him for about a half an hour. And we talked about all of these different things, like the Black Panthers. He had to be a diplomat to stay away from getting involved in that sort of thing because he was also in the U.S. Army at that time. That was his out. I also asked him how it felt to win a tournament like this at a club to which you couldn't belong because of the color of his skin. Asking that question didn't endear me to my fellow members very much, but he said, "I have to go to where the game is played and that someday this will change," and he was right about that. It was great for him and it was great for me because after we left the air I got a phone call from CBS—somebody had seen it, and they asked me to do the U.S. Open.

Then he went to do something that will never be done again, unless there is a radical change in the structure of competitive tennis. Arthur won the U.S. Open to become the only tennis player ever to win the U.S. Amateur and the U.S. Open in the same year. He could do it because he was in the U.S. Army. He wanted to be a pro—he was an advocate for

The horn-rimmed glasses are the first clue that this is Ashe fairly early in his career. Here he returns a shot against Marty Riessen en route to winning the 1967 National Clay Court Tournament in Milwaukee. (AP/Wide World Photos)

open tennis—but he could afford to compete in open tennis as an amateur thanks to his agent Donald Dell, who had found a very obscure regulation in sporting rules concerning Olympians that if you were in the service and training for your country for the Olympics, you could have temporary duty to compete. Dell had researched it thoroughly and thought because the Davis Cup team is also a U.S. team, why can't the same apply to Ashe? And they said, "Why not indeed?" He was a lieutenant in the army, so that way he got to do all this temporary duty (which entails getting paid to travel) and that kept him playing everywhere. He didn't miss much tennis thanks to this allowance, although there were some times he had to be on duty and missed tournaments. The flip side of that, though, meant he could not take prize money at the U.S. Open because the Davis Cup at that time was an amateur vehicle. He couldn't have it both ways.

☙❧

Deford offered this succinct assessment of Ashe's place in American racial history, written soon after Ashe's February 1993 death:

But above all, race was forever crucial to understanding the way in which the world dealt with Arthur Ashe. He was, I came to think, in matters of race, the Universal Soldier, some kind of keystone figure we need if ever brothership is to triumph. He was black, but he perfectly infiltrated white American society as much as he needed to, and even beyond that he was just terribly interested in everybody everywhere in the world.[1]

☙❧

Donald Dell *discovered early on in his relationship with Ashe that Ashe would not kowtow to anyone, black or white, trying to influence his beliefs:*

I remember being in the basement of Andy Young's house in Atlanta in 1968, talking about the black movement, and a young guy called out, "Arthur, you've got to be more outspoken, more aggressive." And he said, "Jesse (Jackson), I'm just not arrogant, and I ain't never going to be arrogant. I'm just going to do it my way."[2]

⁂

Robert Kelleher, *Ashe's first Davis Cup captain, tried to put the reigns on what he perceived as Ashe's penchant for political activism, fearing that Ashe would only get himself into hot water. What he didn't know in the early- to mid-sixties was that Ashe was more than willing at least to put a toe into those hot waters:*

Arthur was an activist in those days and was on his soapbox, such as when he criticized apartheid in South Africa. He was pretty outspoken, using strong words. I was close enough to Arthur at the time, being his senior really, and he sometimes looked to me for advice and my advice was for him to quiet down. I said, "You know, we're going to get you over to South Africa to play in that tournament, and the way you can teach them a lesson is to go over there and beat them." By golly, that's what he did. Arthur went to South Africa as the first black athlete to appear in public in any kind of sport, and in winning the championship, he thereby accomplished an enormous advance in the whole anti-apartheid program.

⁂

Stan Smith discusses the tightrope aspect of Ashe's African-American role in the public eye:

Arthur lived in a white world and he had a lot of white friends. We would talk over issues and he certainly saw the other side of any story, but he was always open-minded. He always had to live two lives—some blacks considered him an Uncle Tom at the same time he was considered a racist by many whites. He was neither, but he was certainly categorized as one or the other by the general public. When he would make a statement supporting a Jesse Jackson or a black activist, the whites would get on his case; but if he would question (another black leader) then the blacks would get on his case. He had the courage to walk that line and was admired by people on both sides. He was arrested in Washington and felt strongly about that.

⚭

Harry Marmion, former USTA president, belonged to a club that was not open to blacks, and it's a club whose exclusionary policies Ashe experienced firsthand in the small world of tennis:

One of the things that Arthur and I spoke about concerned his knowing that I lived in Southampton, New York, and played tennis at the Meadow Club. And we were talking about the time years earlier when he had played the Eastern Grass Court circuit which included East Hampton and Southampton, as well as Philadelphia and South Orange, and then it was back to New York. This was not a happy and easy time for an African American. Well, as Arthur told me, he took a train out of New York for Southampton, got off the train, and took a cab to the Meadow Club, where one of those Easter Grass Court matches was to be played. On his way in he noticed a sign outside the club that said, "Whites Only." But what the sign was referring to, of course, was clothes and how you were supposed to dress for tennis. Still, he said it didn't make him feel good. Then when he got inside the club, they put him in the squash court—they put a lot of cots in there for players—and he didn't get to go to any of the private homes because he felt that nobody wanted him. So it was a very tough deal for him when traveling around. Later on sometime I went back to talk to the man who had been responsible for those tournaments at the club, and I asked him how he dealt with Arthur Ashe when he was coming there to play in the tournaments. And he said, "Well, we were very careful. We put him into the squash court just like we did with anyone else who didn't have a home to stay in." Those were difficult times for Arthur and he triumphed over them very, very well.

I think it was his pacifism that helped him a little bit; however, on the issue of South Africa, it was exactly the opposite, and I talked to him a couple of times about this and how he was going to react if he went down there, and of course he went. He took them on. He took on the establishment and wouldn't play at segregated places. That gets back to the comparisons between Jackie Robinson and Arthur Ashe. Robinson had been a baseball player who had also been a hero in World War II.

Ashe was bigger than life when it came to civil rights. He was a great American emancipator for civil rights long before he became well known as a tennis player. He really was better known as somebody who broke the color line and who then went to South Africa to force the issue with the establishment on racial grounds, and then he just happened to be the first black man to win the U.S. Open and Wimbledon. He had a dual role in life and that was the way all the time, and that's why he was very, very special. Then he won Wimbledon. The people who knew him best as mentors to him, such as Donald Dell and Clark Graebner, were among the ones who saw the goodness in the man and the bravery of the man.

Ashe, who didn't marry until he was in his mid-thirties, dated a number of white women during his bachelor days. As much as he was color blind in terms of deciding what women he liked to be with, his multiracial dating did raise a few eyebrows, as former World Tennis Magazine *publisher* **Gladys Heldman** *recalls:*

For a while, while he was in New York, he dated Chan Aleong, a Chinese girl who worked for me. It was very sweet; a nice relationship for both of them. She was head of circulation for the magazine and a very nice, young, quiet girl, but it was slightly serious. If it was a big romance, I think it was more on her side.

When we lived in Houston and Arthur came to stay with us, he asked if he could bring a girlfriend. Of course we said yes. And he brought a Canadian woman, a very attractive blonde, and they got along very well. We had several other houseguests at the same time. A couple of things happened. First, a local Houstonian asked us to a dinner party she was giving at a very nice club called the Bayou Club in Houston, and she wanted us to bring our houseguests, including Arthur. And I told her that Arthur has a girl with him and our hostess thought for a minute and then said that was fine, "Bring her, too." Remember, tradition was very strong at that time in Houston, and I think it was the first time that a black had ever been invited to the Bayou Club, other than the waiters. Then our hostess did a double take when she saw who Arthur's date was, and while that surprised her, she handled it very well. All prejudices were lost very quickly.

⚬⟋⟍⟋⟍⟍⟋

Christine Beck, one of Ashe's Philadelphia-based associates for the development of youth tennis, says that race defined Ashe's legacy, even with everything else that had gone on in his life:

I think it was tougher for him than I'll ever know. I remember him saying, even after he had contracted AIDS, that the greatest burden he had ever had to bear was race—his being black. He was concerned at times in his life about being labeled an Uncle Tom because he did want to do it all. But he questioned many things and wouldn't always take things at face value.

⚬⟋⟍⟋⟍⟍⟋

The most memorable brief period of Ashe's life probably occurred in 1973 when he was finally given a visa to South Africa and then played in that year's South African Open. Critics from both sides of South Africa's apartheid system vehemently opposed Ashe's trip to South Africa, and he certainly understood and accepted the ramifications of his controversial visit. Ashe later admitted he often felt in physical danger while he was in South Africa and he was followed as he traveled throughout the country. **Donald Dell** *explains:*

Arthur and I went to Vietnam twice. Arthur and Stan went to Africa. I flew down and negotiated for Arthur to go to South Africa with a cabinet member who would later become their prime minister. Arthur had been turned down three times for a visa because previously he had declared in a press interview that "Because of apartheid, I would like to drop a hydrogen bomb on Johannesburg." Arthur and I used to talk about it and laugh about it, and I would tell him "Arthur, they're not going to give you a visa under those circumstances." After he had been turned down three times in something like two years, he really wanted to go more than ever because he was just curious—he wanted to go see the country and see what it was like. So I negotiated with the official and got them to agree to invite Arthur to the tennis tournament down there in Johannesburg. It was conditional and we didn't really announce the terms, but the conditions for Arthur to be permitted to go there were very specific: he could do press conferences, go anywhere, do anything, and play in the tennis tournament—all on one condition: that while he was physically in the territory of South Africa, he would not use press conferences to attack the government and the country, but would rather talk about tennis and the tournament and all that. However, before he went into the country and after he came out of the country, he was free to do or say anything that he wanted. It was sort of like a political gag order, but because he was in the tennis tournament, he had a perfect excuse to say, "I'm just going to be here to play tennis, blah, blah, blah."

Blacks in South Africa were very split on his coming—
half liked it and half hated it. He got letters and threats and
everything imaginable. Some of the militant blacks were
asking, "What in the hell are you doing here? You're not crit-
icizing the country. You're not saying crap about the government, and this is hurting us, and you're like an Uncle Tom."
The other side of the argument, which Arthur showed, was
that he got to the finals of the tournament and lost to
Connors in four sets. It showed a lot of the blacks of South
Africa that they weren't inferior, that they could compete.
There are a lot of things that you and I couldn't imagine
because we're not black, and particularly because we're not
South African black—when you've been told from day one
that you're a dummy and you're inferior and all the different
things you are, that you are a different type of citizen, you
don't have equal say, and you don't have equal citizenship
under apartheid. The fact that he came and talked to people
and did all the things that he did, to include going to see
Nelson Mandela on Robbins Island, I mean he did a helluva
lot of things that were very controversial, but he didn't crit-
icize anybody.

When he got out, I can remember we wrote a press
release while flying back from Johannesburg to New York,
where we had a huge two-hour press conference after we
landed. He really blasted them (the South African government), but he did it in Arthur's typical fashion, with an
intellectual well-reasoned statement, not yelling and
screaming. In this way he was the antithesis of (Al)
Sharpton, for example. Arthur was very much an intellectual. He was a speed reader with a photographic memory
who had a tremendously high IQ, and he just wasn't going to
indulge in the screaming and shouting with all the ranting

and raving. He would say things very articulately and very quietly.

⌒∞∞⌒

Deford was among the reporters who accompanied Ashe on his 1973 trip to South Africa:

It was pretty tense in South Africa. A lot of people didn't want Arthur to go. It wasn't like, "Oh, hooray, Arthur is going to break the color line." There were a lot of people who felt that he was giving in to the South African government; that they were using him. I can remember flying over and joining him in London. He was meeting with a guy named Dennis Brutus, who I already knew, and Dennis was what they call a "colored" in South Africa. A mulatto. And coloreds were considered different than blacks. Brutus had been a South African colored and had gotten out, and he didn't want Arthur to go. He was running an organization and was trying to talk him out of it. I mean, this was at the last minute with the plane on the runway and there's Brutus arguing with Arthur, not letting him out of the hotel, although I don't mean physically. Arthur finally says, "I know they're using me, but I'm using them, too." We did manage to make the plane.

There were a lot of people who felt that way. By then, Arthur was a student of South Africa. By the time he went there, Arthur knew more about South Africa than did 99 percent of the people living in South Africa. That was the way he went about things. When Arthur got interested in something, he grabbed onto it like a dog with a bone. He would grab onto it with his teeth and just clench onto it.

That's what he did in this case: he studied South African history, South African geography, South African culture—not just simple race relations, everything. I remember on the plane a guy came up to him, a white South African, who wished him well and said something to the effect that "We're not all that way. I'm so glad you're here and good luck."

While over there we stayed at an estate, which had been given to us to use by a white South African. Arthur and I stayed in rooms next to each other and we shared a bathroom. That's how close we were, and every day we would talk about things. I was sort of his eyes and ears to the white world and then he would tell me things. We compared notes every night. It was altogether fascinating. It was really history in the making, and I don't mean just somebody winning his twelfth straight game or something like that. It also went without incident. There was no ugliness. We always knew we were being followed, but that was as much for Arthur's protection as anything else. It wasn't like anyone was out to get him. The South Africans certainly did not want any kind of incident.

I remember while we were over there we met with a guy named Don Mattera, a poet who was what they called "banned." You couldn't speak, you couldn't print. To meet with somebody who was banned was extraordinary because it told you what really a totalitarian government South Africa had. You couldn't talk to anybody, you couldn't print anything, you had no public life whatsoever. You were a nonperson. That was very striking, especially to me being a journalist. I mean, what would it be like if someone were to cut my tongue out, figuratively?

In the tournament, where he got to the finals, the guy he played in the semis was a white South African, Cliff Drysdale who is now an announcer for ESPN and was a very good friend of Arthur's. Cliff was also totally in favor of the end of apartheid. It was a very dramatic match and Arthur beat Drysdale but then he got beat by Connors in the final. Arthur couldn't stand Connors, and that had nothing to do with race—it was tennis politics. Arthur had been a part of the tennis players' union, and Connors wouldn't join. Connors ended up whipping his butt, but that set up the great victory over Connors the next year at Wimbledon. I didn't go to Wimbledon that year, but I just about died when I found out that Arthur had won because I didn't think he could do anything with Connors. Arthur really wanted to win that.

After the (South African) tournament was over, we traveled around the country some. At one point in the trip, Arthur had a debate against a professor from a place called Stellenbosch, which is sort of the Harvard University of South Africa. This professor was arguing on behalf of apartheid and Arthur, of course, was arguing against it. It was a very intellectual, civil conversation. The guy was presenting his point of view and Arthur was giving at least as good as he got. Of course, I was prejudiced to favoring Arthur's side. At one point, Arthur pointed down at this old black guy and said, "Why can't this gentleman vote and you can? Explain that to me." And it was funny because he just took the wind out of the guy's sails. When you put it on that sort of personal level, all the guy could say was, "I can't answer that, Mr. Ashe." That was really dramatic.

⚬⚬⚬⚬

Even Ashe's precise skin color was a subject some deemed worthy of examination during his South African journey, as pointed out by a South African newspaper:

Perhaps the biggest surprise is that he is not black at all. The pigmentation of the player who represents blacks in world tennis is more brown or Oriental yellow.[3]

Dennis Ralston *remembers talking about race with Ashe and having empathy for his comrade's unique place in the tennis world:*

I always thought we were pretty good friends. We went through a lot of difficult times together. In the sixties we weren't sure where he stood on racial issues. He was the only black in an otherwise all-white sport and he had some hang-ups about that. I remember one time when we were in Champagne, Illinois, and out of the blue he asked me, "Denny, how would you feel if Angela (Ralston's daughter) dated a black guy?" And I said, "Well, I don't know, but how would you feel if you had a daughter and she wanted to date a white guy?" He was dating white girls and black girls at the time, so it's something he was thinking about a lot of the time.

It was difficult for the rest of us to understand what Arthur was going through trying to fit in. He knew that he would not be able to get in a lot of tennis clubs unless he was a tennis player, but he grew to realize that everybody was a person. Had to be tough to be first black tennis player since Althea Gibson, but everybody on the tour treated him equally and there were no racial issues among them. He was

Ashe going for a backhand against Jimmy Connors in the 1975 singles final at Wimbledon. (AP/Wide World Photos)

just another player. We were pretty far apart politically. He knew I didn't come into the sport with a silver spoon in my mouth. I came from a very middle-class family, low income, and I got to where I did through a lot of hard work as things weren't just handed to me. I knew he was trying to deal with the apartheid mess and there were groups telling him to boycott this or not to do that, things that the rest of us would not have to worry about.

꼿꼿

Ashe and race were two subjects joined at the hip long before Ashe even applied for a visa to South Africa, as **Deford** *remembers:*

Nineteen sixty-eight was a time of real racial turmoil. That was the year that (medallist sprinters) Tommy Smith and John Carlos gave the black power salute at the Olympics, and it was the same year that Lew Alcindor wouldn't even go into the Olympics. It was also the year that Bobby Kennedy and Martin Luther King Jr. were assassinated. The context in what Arthur did that year, winning the U.S. Open, was amazing. That, the South African trip in 1973, and winning Wimbledon in 1975 are what marked Arthur Ashe as an athlete.

꼿꼿

Ashe never second-guessed his decision in 1973 to visit South Africa, a move that was as much about apartheid as it was about playing there in a tennis tournament:

South Africa was testing the credibility of Western civilization. If you didn't come out against the most corrupt system imaginable, you couldn't look yourself in the eye.[4]

꼿꼿

The following excerpt from a 1992 Sports Illustrated *article that appeared in the issue announcing Ashe as that year's* SI Sportsman *of the Year sets the tone for the political significance of Ashe's visit to South Africa in 1973:*

When Ashe traveled to South Africa to play in the 1973 South African Open, he met journalist and poet Don Mattera, a black native of the country who at first was critical of Ashe's visit, claiming the African American was unwittingly playing into the hands of the apartheid national government. But Ashe made a convincing argument to counter Mattera's viewpoint and cited Dr. Martin Luther King Jr. and Frederick Douglass in showing how the struggle against racism can be a peaceful one taken one step at a time. Ashe made an impact on Mattera as evidenced by the following poem that Mattera composed soon after his meeting with Ashe. A few days after Mattera met Ashe, he was declared a nonperson by the South African Bureau of State Security, meaning he could not publish, travel, or have a discussion with more than two people at a time. Mattera penned his tribute to Ashe late at night at his home after putting his six children to bed, writing by the light of a single candle that he lit:

> I listened deeply when you spoke
> About the step-by-step evolution
> Of a gradual harvest,
> Tendered by the rains of tolerance
> And patience.
> Your youthful face,
> A mask,
> Hiding a pining, anguished spirit,

And I loved you brother—
Not for your quiet philosophy
But for the rage in your soul,
Trained to be rebuked or summoned . . . [5]

∽∾∽

It wasn't enough for Ashe that he lived for the now in doing his part to work toward equal rights for blacks around the world, he also felt the need for knowing more about the heritage of African-American athletes. Dismayed, however, when he couldn't find any books or resource material that qualified as a consummate study of African Americans in sports, he set out to do the work himself. The result was a three-volume series titled A Hard Road to Glory *that was published in 1988:*

When I researched *Hard Road*, I wondered, given the richness of our heritage, why no Ph.D. type had written it. Then I realized that the study of the sociology and history of black sports wasn't thought to be career advancing. The academic glamour, the appeal, was in civil rights. But man, was there power in sports.[6]

∽∾∽

Former tennis professional and current USTA officer **Rodney Harmon** *always looked up to Ashe not only for his tennis play but for his bold stance on African-American issues:*

They don't make them like Arthur anymore, someone who suffered a lot and then wants to help others the way he did. He was selfless in that he would take on unpopular causes, like the whole South Africa thing. He would take on all these causes that he felt were important and were outside the realm of sports. He wanted to be involved with them because that's what he felt he should be doing, and that's what he felt strongly about. But then to do all that and still be one of the most talented players ever, to have won Wimbledon and the U.S. Open, to have been top five in the world . . . it's amazing. You might get someone who's a great activist and not a great athlete, or vice versa, and then you get Arthur who achieved so much in sports and still gave back so much for various causes as an activist. It's like, "When do you rest?" He would listen, just listen. I remember him talking about South Africa and how he thought that by going he would help open up the world's eyes to what was going on, but as it turned out it really didn't make a difference. "Everything would seem fine for the time that I was there," Arthur said, "but the situation for blacks who were poor never really changed. When I left, it was business as usual." Things did eventually change in South Africa, but it took some time.

⌒∞∞⌒

Following Ashe's February 1993 death, Time *magazine published this testimonial to him:*

Of the protean figures responsible for the integration of sports in America, Ashe stood in the first rank. Jesse Owens proved that white men do not run faster or jump farther than blacks. Jackie Robinson disproved with a fiery passion that whites have a stronger desire to win. Muhammad Ali demonstrated in the ring that speed and power were the only obvious ways in which a black athlete could be agile and courageous. There have been other pathfinders: decathlete

Milt Campbell, golfer Charlie Sifford, and in Ashe's own sport the lithe and graceful Althea Gibson.

But none of them possessed the combination of attributes that made Ashe a paradigm of understated reason and elegance. In 1973 Ashe went off to play in the South African Open to see if he could chip away at the foundation of apartheid. Militants in the African National Congress did not welcome the visit, castigating him as an Uncle Tom and telling him he should go home. Ashe listened and replied evenly, "Small concessions incline toward larger ones."[7]

✎

Eliot Teltscher, like Harmon another former tennis player personally familiar with Ashe, also brings up Jackie Robinson in evaluating Ashe's place in tennis history:

If you compare what Arthur did for tennis to what Jackie Robinson did for baseball, you've got to remember that at the time Robinson broke Major League Baseball's color line, there already were lots of blacks playing baseball. Sure, they weren't playing with white players, they were segregated. But many were playing the game, and at a high level. In tennis, however, for the most part there just weren't any, or at least many, blacks playing tennis. There just weren't. It wasn't like there was a separate black league for tennis players like there was for baseball, or even for golf. That's why what Arthur was able to do was that much more difficult. I'm not trying to belittle Jackie Robinson or what he did by saying it wasn't a tremendous accomplishment—it was. But he was already playing in a very high level of baseball competition with other blacks before he came to the major leagues. There wasn't a comparable black tennis league for Arthur. Tennis for the most part was something that white people played at white tennis clubs.

Things are starting to change, and that's because the world is changing. It is still very difficult for African Americans to get into tennis, but it is slowly starting to change. In Arthur's time, it was really, really difficult. I have to think that what he accomplished and starting way back in the sixties, especially, had to be close to impossible. He was a stand-up guy. The thing I remember about Arthur was that the way he transcended history was so difficult.

ও᙭᙭ৎ

Ashe never automatically went along with actions driven by racial hatred, as he was quoted as saying in the December 21, 1992, issue of Sports Illustrated:

Each of us comes up with his or her own social contracts, agreements with our group or our nation, or just ourselves. Those Crips and Bloods, those kids who showed no remorse (after truckdriver Reginald Denny was beaten during riots in Los Angeles), had no contract with America, just with raw, primeval, individual survival.[8]

ও᙭᙭ৎ

A sense of humor gave Ashe the capacity to laugh off racial misconceptions and references, as **Gladys Heldman** *points out:*

I remember the time that they were having a Calcutta at River Oaks in Houston, and this was a club where only men could be members of River Oaks, provided they were Anglo.

Arthur was dressed casually for the event but very nicely. He got up to make a speech and said, "I never thought I would be up here to be sold again." Arthur had dignity and he could be funny.

⚭

4

TRUSTING FRIEND

Arthur Ashe was not a gregarious person nor was he shallow. He didn't surround himself with large entourages to run interference for him. Yet, as accessible as he was in public, he was a private man intensely loyal to a select number of acquaintances. Potential friends didn't so much flock to him as they were in fact brought to him through circumstances and then tested over time as to their reliability and honesty. It wasn't that Ashe was arrogant or untrusting; it's just that he was very careful in determining whom he would welcome into his inner circle. But once you were a friend of Ashe's, the give and take of that relationship was genuinely warm and mutual.

Ashe played most of his career on the international tennis circuit at a time when friendships between players, and even between athletes and journalists, were fostered—the latter match something that would be taboo in today's adversarial world that puts the media on one end of the rope and oft-coddled, untrusting sports stars on the other. If you were one of Ashe's friends, he knew your children's names, remembered your birthday, and was comfortable enough with you to share a great sense of humor not evident in a public persona that appeared as stoic as it was studious.

Ashe did not discriminate between black and white when it came to making friends. His most important personal, as well as professional, relationship was with Donald Dell, a white man. When he was a bachelor, Ashe was as likely to be found courting a white woman as an African-American woman. If anyone didn't like that, that was their problem, not his. At the same time, Ashe didn't turn his back on his roots. He aggressively worked for decades for causes that would help educate young blacks while introducing them to tennis. One of his long-time proteges was fellow African-American tennis player Rodney Harmon, who would reach the quarterfinals of the 1982 U.S. Open.

That Ashe was a man who inspired trust in his closest associates and friends was demonstrated when Ashe learned in 1988 he was HIV positive, resulting from tainted blood that he received in a blood transfusion following his second heart attack in the early eighties. Ashe told several friends but asked them to keep it quiet, which they did for several years, even amid swirling rumors that something was seriously wrong with Ashe's health. The secret was a burden to bear, but it was done for the sake of one of America's most prominent citizens.

༺༻

Ashe was loyal to friends he trusted, and there were more than a handful, which he also meant he was willing to hear whatever they had to say as long as the open communications worked both ways, as fellow tennis player **Stan Smith** *explains:*

It was always interesting with Arthur, in part because he could be so unpredictable at times. One time, out of the blue, he said to me, "Guess what book I am reading now." That was kind of an odd thing to say because of the way it came out of nowhere when we had been talking about something completely different. And, likewise, out of the blue I answered, "The Bible." Surprised, he said, "How did you know?" I guess by this time he knew that I was a Christian. I had talked to him some about my faith, and that was because I was always concerned with seeing where he stood on the issue of faith. This was after he had a heart attack and was having some physical problems, which is why I was especially concerned about the issue of faith and him. Knowing this, he was kind of excited about the fact that he was reading his Bible, and he wanted me to know about that. That was a special moment for both of us, and he spent a lot of time during the last three or four years of his life being around Christians. Near the end of Arthur's life there was a minister in New York with whom Arthur spent a lot of time, and, of course, he was friends with Andrew Young (an ordained minister, too). In the end I think Arthur made a commitment to Christianity, but he still considered himself a citizen of the world and a man of all faiths. He studied the Muslims and certainly had an interest in people like Muhammad Ali who made a switch to the Muslim faith. There were times that Arthur and I had some nice talks about different faiths. I remember his thinking that no matter what faith people adhered to, everybody was the same. Still, again, in the end I think he realized that there was a difference between Christianity and the other faiths. For most of his life I think he saw all these faiths as pretty much the same, but just involving different cultures.

❦

Another of Ashe's closest friends was **Donald Dell,** *the tennis-player-turned-attorney-turned-agent. Dell was a mover and shaker in the worlds of politics and tennis. But before becoming Ashe's agent, Dell had tried to link Ashe up with a certain Harvard Business School grad who was well on his way to becoming the world's number one sports agent:*

Arthur figured, from my days with Bobby Kennedy and my having worked at the Office of Economic Opportunity, that he couldn't, in the mind of a young black athlete, be with anybody with better credentials than that. I had lived it. We had been raising money all over the country for poor blacks and OEO, which Republicans hated because they thought we were building a Democratic power house of young voters. That was not the plan or program at all, but they feared that, so they cut the budgets and the funding after Shriver got out.

I think I had an ability to communicate with Arthur that was built on trust and friendship, however that evolved. By way of example, Arthur and I had our own separate language. When I really wanted to get his attention in a meeting, I'd call him "Lieutenant." We had certain buzzwords that were just instinctive. He had been very helpful to a guy named Ron Charity in Virginia who had stiffed Arthur on a

$30,000 loan. Ron Charity had helped teach Arthur how to play tennis back in Virginia, so he wouldn't let me sue him. This was years later, after Arthur had turned pro.

When Arthur went to turn pro and had seen the front cover of my book (*Minding Other People's Business*), I took Arthur to see Mark McCormack not once, but four times. McCormack had started IMG (International Management Group), which is a great sports marketing company. After the third or fourth time of going to see McCormack, and this was while we were riding in a cab, he said, "How many more times are you going to do that?" And I said, "Do what?" He said, "Taking me to Mark McCormack. He's kind of aloof and not very friendly, and I don't want to see him anymore." I said, "Fine. I just thought that he could do the best job for you. He's got Jean-Claude Killy and the golfers Jack Nicklaus, Arnold Palmer, and Gary Player. He's a reputable guy and I thought he could make you the most money, but do whatever you want." We continued on riding along in this cab, and then he turns to me and says, "Well, why don't you do it?" And I said, "Do what?" "Be my lawyer and manager." And I said, "No, Arthur. I'm going back to Washington to work for Hogan and Hartson to become the next Clarence Darrow. Why would I want to do all this crap?" He said, "Look, I'm serious. If you will just be my lawyer, then Stan (Smith) will join us, and we can build a little business and help you do it."

I wasn't really planning to do it, but as things unfolded when I went back and told the senior partner at Hogan and Hartson, they got so excited that they offered me a whole floor and tax people and accountants and everything else, and I suddenly realized that maybe this was something that I should look into. That's how I started Pro-Serve. I told Arthur I would do it, and he called Stan, and Stan agreed to do it. They became my first two clients. As it turned out, McCormack couldn't close the deal with Arthur even with my help. That was kind of a funny thing and people teased Mark about it for a long time because Ashe was such a big name.

❦

Veteran scribe **Frank Deford** *met Ashe in the early sixties and over the years developed a friendship that was about as strong as any relationship between journalist and covered athlete can be:*

I first met Arthur when he was at UCLA, which I think was also my first year at *Sports Illustrated.* He was about three years younger than I was. People knew about him because he had a bright promise, but mostly because he was the first prominent male black player. He certainly wasn't famous or anything like that at that stage, and I certainly wasn't well-known as a writer then. We met each other and really got to like each other, just as friends. I wasn't really covering him yet as a journalist. The friendship simply grew and eventually it did involve the journalistic thing because of a cover piece on him I did for *Sports Illustrated.* By the time he left UCLA, people were getting interested in him and he eventually moved up to number two or three in the country. Dennis Ralston was still the premier American player tennis player at that time, and then there was a guy named Chuck McKinley. Those guys were one and two.

❦

*As **Smith** remembers it, Ashe's concern for the people he truly cared about was a driving force in their friendship:*

One of Arthur's strong points was the genuine empathy he had for people, yet it was nothing that he ever made a big deal out of. That just wasn't his style. The fact that he himself went through some tough times in terms of being mistreated when playing at clubs is one reason why he had empathy towards others. One time we were playing at a tournament in Sydney, which was one of the biggest tournaments of the year, only for me to lose in the first round. Not only was it a big tournament, I was hoping to win it, not just do well. Because I was pretty serious about the match, I took the loss sort of hard. And Arthur wasn't oblivious to how I felt. A little later he wrote me a note and dropped it off at my room, encouraging me to hang in there. We were travelling the tour together and stuff like this happens all of the time, but this was an especially significant time and Arthur realized it was a discouraging loss for me. I don't know if ever there was another time he did something like that for another player, but I wouldn't be surprised. Keep in mind that while all this was going on for me in Sydney he was working on his own game and trying to win the tournament as well, but then he would do things that certainly meant a lot on a personal level. Sure, what he did for others were small things in a way, but they were meaningful and significant, obviously important to whomever he was trying to help.

⚬▬▬▬⚬

Deford delves more into the development of his friendship with Ashe, which wasn't an overnight deal:

There are some people you click with, and Arthur and I clicked. One thing you've got to remember about the sixties is that athletes and writers back then had a tendency to be much friendlier with each other than they are now. You've got to put it in the context of the times. I was friendly with a lot of tennis players. Another thing is that Arthur and I had a lot of the same interests. For one thing, ironically, my mother's side of the family had come from Richmond. We speculated that there were people in his family who might have worked for my mother's family. That sort of thing interested Arthur. Also, we weren't far apart in age.

He also had the most amazing facility for being able to remember the names of people's wives and children, and I'm so awful at that, and he probably knew twenty times more people than I did. I can still see him going up to someone and saying, "How's Bill? How's Mary?" He was such a sweet guy. One time we were up at the Newport Casino playing there and he comes off the court, hands his racket to my son, who was probably twelve years old at the time, and did that without any thought of that. My son is thirty-one now and he still has that racket. That was just Arthur's way. He cared about people, and he was a wonderful human being.

I think people have turned Arthur into a saint by now, and he deserves all that, but he also had a great sense of humor. He was a very funny guy to be with. That's another reason I liked him. We could always laugh and joke together.

᪐ᵔᵔᵔᵔᵔᵔᵔᵔᵔᵔ᪐

Deford collaborated with Ashe in writing the book Arthur
Ashe: Portrait in Motion, *which is a one-year diary of Ashe's
that encompasses the year between the 1973 and 1974
Wimbledon tournaments. During that time, Ashe made 129 air-
plane trips covering five continents and 165,000 miles, during
which time he slept in 71 different beds:*

When Arthur decided he was going to do that book, I guess
I was the logical person to do it with him. I was just
delighted. By then we really knew each other very well, and
he had already won the U.S. Open. Not only that, about two
years before that, Arthur went to Africa on a state department tour and I went with him to do an article for *Sports
Illustrated.* It was Arthur, me, Stan Smith, Bud Collins, a
British writer named Richard Evans, and Donald Dell. We
traveled all over Africa, going to about six or seven countries
such as Tanzania, Zambia, Uganda, and Nigeria. We were in
Africa together for about two weeks in all. Although I was
there doing an article, the best way to put it was that it was
more a matter of just us hanging out. So by the time Arthur
and I did the book, Arthur and I were pretty good friends.

I lived in New York then, and he had moved to New
York. The way we started off the book was that he was going
to write into a diary every day, but that didn't work because it
turned out to involve too much writing in longhand for him.
We didn't have computers then. Gosh, I can remember that
so well. What we did was, he would tape his thoughts every
night into a recorder and then send me the tape. A tape
would arrive every three weeks. Plus we would see each other
fairly regularly too, so it wasn't like this was done just by
tapes. The main thing with the tapes, I told him, was, "Look,
you don't have to get everything down. Just get enough down

so that I can then follow up and ask you things like, "What about this?" or "What about that?" And from that, you could flesh it out. He was pretty good. Typical of Arthur, he was very dedicated to this project. And then I'd occasionally see him while traveling around. One time we went to Montreal together for a doubles tournament, and we also went to Wimbledon together. There were two or three other short little trips that we made, and then in the fall we went to South Africa where he broke the color line. Now that was really extraordinary. That still is the most significant thing I have been a part of as a journalist.

⟳⟳⟳

Tom Okker, of the Netherlands, shared with Ashe an abiding love of art, which is proof positive that tennis players, at least those in the sixties and seventies, actually spent enough time away from the tennis court to get to know each other and each other's interests well:

I got to know him pretty well. I think it was in 1969 that we went on an African tour with Charlie Pasarell and his wife, Arthur and his girlfriend, and Marty Riessen and his wife, and there was me with my wife. We went to West Africa for a couple of weeks and ended up in Kenya, where we went on a safari trip, so yeah, we did a few things together. He stayed at my house a couple of times and we played doubles a few times in some big events, so we were pretty good friends.

We also played doubles together in tournaments a number of times. The biggest event in which we played doubles was when we were in South Africa playing in a tournament. We won the doubles there in a finals match that was sort of unusual from the standpoint that you were supposed to wear white clothes in matches, especially in South Africa. Well, when we played on the center court, we went out there dressed in these big red-and-white-striped shirts courtesy of a clothing contract with Catalina. But the kicker is that we didn't show them until after we had played one game. We had our track suits on, and after the first game we both took off the tops of our track suits to reveal the red and white shirts. The crowd cheered because they loved it, so that was a good memory. It was just something we thought was fun and a little bit provocative, of course. We also had some blue shirts, green shirts, and yellow shirts that we could have worn.

⚭

DD Eisenberg *was another journalist who found that the dynamics of being a professional reporter covering a professional athlete need not be a deterrent to being a friend to someone you covered, which is a phenomenon pretty much taboo in today's world of confrontational reporting:*

Back in the seventies I was the first woman sports reporter (for a major daily newspaper, the *Philadelphia Bulletin*) in Philadelphia and covered all kinds of sports because they didn't know what to do with me. Eventually, though, the tennis reporter left and I got the beat. I covered other sports, but tennis was the one that I concentrated on. That was during the era of Stan Smith, Marty Riessen, Arthur, Jimmy Connors, and Roscoe Tanner. I would go and cover the Open and Wimbledon and other tournaments that were nearby. Whenever Arthur was in a tournament, he was always the one I wanted to interview because his comments were poignant and very quotable.

As a reporter, you would go to ask him questions and after thirty to forty-five minutes with him, he would be asking you questions about things that had nothing to do with what the article was about. He was always learning from other people. I liked that about him. He was a sensitive and observant person. That's what made him so special. He expected a lot of everyone and he could get testy if he thought you had asked a stupid question or you hadn't done your homework. Still, he wouldn't be as nasty as some of the other players could be. He kept his cool. I think I've patterned a lot of things I've done in my life over the last twenty years after him. He has served as a serious role model for me, and hopefully I have passed along some of his more giving traits to others.

First I got to know him as a professional, but then I started getting involved in Philadelphia Youth Tennis, which was then called the Philadelphia Tennis Patrons Association. I was on the board. One of the first decisions we made was to name the building after Arthur. He would come every year for our big benefit, and from his association and commitment we were able to get other celebrities such as Frank Deford, Chris Evert, Mary Carillo, Bud Collins, and all of Arthur's cronies. It grew from maybe 200 or 300 to 900 or a thousand with a waiting list.

As a journalist, the last thing I wanted to be considered was a fundraiser, but Arthur would keep encouraging me in that capacity because he knew how important it was to stage a first-class event that was successful. Even if it was something he didn't like to do, he believed in the organization and what we were trying to do. This was his way of giving back, by helping to bring in the money that provided funds for the youth programs. We would usually have this event on a weeknight so that he could be home for the weekends. Balancing a family life was always a top priority for Arthur.

◦〜◦

*Another of Ashe's close friends the last fifteen years of his life was **Seth Abraham,** the president of HBO Sports, where Ashe ended up working starting in the early eighties:*

I had met him socially at events in the seventies, at various sports events and just snippets of exchanges, but I very much admired him. HBO televised Wimbledon and I always had it in my mind he would be a remarkable broadcaster for HBO—tennis as well as other things we might be able to find for him. Very early in my administration—I joined HBO in 1978—I made two efforts to hire Arthur through Donald Dell, who was Arthur's lawyer/agent and also probably his best friend. It was frustrating because Arthur had a contract with ABC. At that point, I asked Donald to provide me with a much-longer introduction, and Arthur and I started meeting. We started with a breakfast, and inch by inch, foot by foot, yard by yard, it became a friendship. Finally, in the early eighties, ABC changed their contract—they had cut way back on their tennis coverage—and at that point became nonexclusive, and we just signed him and grabbed him, in either 1981 or 1982. So now I got to spend summers with him in Wimbledon and traveled with him, so the friendship blossomed because he was now working with me at HBO and we got to spend a lot of time together, including vacation time with our respective families.

◦〜◦

Abraham expands on his take of Ashe and their friendship, one that was as genuine as it was meaningful for both:

Arthur was incredibly loyal. Once you were with him, you were with him forever, and if you wanted to speak to the people in his life—his wife, daughter, friends—you would find he didn't collect people as trophies. Athletes and celebrities in the public eye very often collect hangers-on, barnacles, just because people want to be around famous people. That never interested Arthur: He was looking for something much greater and much deeper. He didn't want to be friends with everybody he met. He wanted to be friends with a group of people that added to his life, and he to theirs, and he was just remarkably loyal to this group of people and often demonstrated it in different ways.

During the week of the U.S. Open in the late eighties, Arthur and I were scheduled one day to meet for lunch and spend the day. I go out there and no Arthur. I called his office, which was at home, and I got a machine; I called my office and they hadn't heard from him. I wasn't overly concerned, but it was a little odd, but things sometimes come up. It was a Friday, the day of the women's semifinals. About three-thirty I'm at the phone bank again calling to find out where Arthur is and I run into David Dinkins, the mayor of New York City and a great friend of Arthur's. I said, "Mr. Mayor, have you heard from Arthur?" And he said, "Oh, haven't you heard? He's in the hospital." I said, "What!?" And he said, "Yeah, he had another incident," as in heart attack or palpitations. He said he was at Cornell, where his cardiologist practiced. At least now I knew where he was, and Mayor Dinkins assured me that he was okay. It had happened the night before and Arthur had just walked over to the hospital.

So now it's about 11:30 Friday night, and I'm at home. The phone rings, and it's Arthur. He's in the critical care unit at Cornell, and he says to me, "I'm really sorry that I didn't meet you, but I'm fine and I'll be discharged in a couple of days." He said, "Now, I need for you to do me a big favor," and I said, "Arthur, anything." He said, "You know, I have tickets tomorrow for Super Saturday"—women's final, men's semis; one of the great tickets in sports—"and I don't want them to go to waste. Would you take them?" I said, "Arthur, you've just head a heart attack and are in the critical-care unit of the hospital, and you're worried about your blankety-blank tickets?" And he said, "Yeah, I didn't want them to go to waste and I knew you could use them." There he is in the critical-care unit and somebody had smuggled in a phone for him, and he's calling to make sure his tickets don't go to waste and that instead they will give somebody pleasure. That to me is a vintage Arthur Ashe story.

ᐧᐧᐧ

Pam Shriver, herself a former tennis pro, got to know Ashe fairly well from the tennis telecasts they did together for ABC:

The times I really got to know him came when we both worked for ABC in the booth covering tennis. Back in the late eighties and early nineties, ABC had a handful of tennis events, such as the Lipton tournament down in Miami and the finals of the tour championship in Madison Square

Garden, as well as a couple other special events in the course of a year. The broadcasting crew was Cliff Drysdale, Arthur, and myself. Arthur was very knowledgeable about tennis, certainly, and he was very professional in how he went about doing his job. He would say a few things that would make you laugh.

I can remember one broadcast—and this is when you have three in the booth and two doing a color role, you will know what the other person is going to say. A couple of times during this broadcast I would start to say something and Arthur knew where I was going with it, and so he would sort of finish some of my statements for me. Finally, one time I nudged him with my elbow and kind of looked at him, and he gave me a look that said, "Yeah, I got it." But then again, it's a natural thing when you're in a conversation with somebody and you know where they're going with something and you sort of interrupt to finish what they are saying.

The only part of a show that is really rehearsed is the opening, and that's because once the players get out there and start playing, all you can do is respond to what's happening out there on court, along with discussing their tendencies in different situations. He had played in an earlier era than I did, so I would feel that I might be able to tell him more about the current players because still in those days I had already played a lot against many of the current players we were covering on television. But Arthur was very astute and able to figure things out pretty quickly on his own, just by watching a game or two. I can't remember a specific one-liner he came up with. But I do remember one time we were up in the booth covering a match with Michael Chang and he had a funny way of praising Chang's lob. He said something like "Michael has the best lob on the planet," and coming from Arthur it came across as kind of a cute comment.

He was a lot of fun to deal with. You could talk to him about serious things, and we would talk sometimes when we had a long break between production meetings and the time when we went on the air. Only God knows where a conversation with him would sometimes take you, and a lot of the time it would be about anything other than tennis.

ଙ୍ଗ୍ୟୁଡ

With Ashe, there always was something to talk about, and
Smith *said that occasionally meant a discussion on politics:*

We talked about politics a number of times. I remember one time he said that he thought he could be president of the United States, which was another example of one of those weird statements that he would sometimes make out of the blue. During the last ten years of his life he did have a tremendous platform from which to speak with his leadership role in tennis and involvement in various causes. Certainly he was very intelligent, and I think he could have been a good politician. But I don't know exactly where that statement came from. Maybe that was his way of speaking his mind and saying, "I would be a good politician." I don't know. Maybe he was just testing me to see what my reaction would be.

ଙ୍ଗ୍ୟୁଡ

Eisenberg *found out just how much Ashe cared about people—
to include reporters he considered his friends—after she gave
birth to her first child:*

I remember back to one time when I was pregnant—it was
1977—and I had to write one of those long articles about
him for a tennis magazine. I had the baby two months early
and no one had really known that I was pregnant because I
hadn't told anyone. I don't know what my problem was, but
maybe it had something to do with my thinking that because
I was a sports writer I wasn't supposed to get pregnant. I had
the baby at seven months. I remember being at home afterward using a breast pump, trying to keep a connection with

*Ashe with several of the women who were long-time cohorts of his in the tennis
world. From left to right are DD Eisenberg, Ashe, Billie Jean King, and
Christine Beck. (Photo courtesy of DD Eisenberg)*

my baby who was to spend five more weeks at the hospital before coming home. I had had surgery and now here I was typing away on my old-fashioned typewriter.

I called Arthur and was trying to write at the same time I interviewed him because I was on deadline. Finally, he says, "You don't sound very good. What's wrong?" And I told him that I had had this baby two months early, and he goes, "Baby! What do you mean you had a baby? You shouldn't be doing this story." And I said, "You know, you would make me feel much better and less stressed out if you would just let me finish talking to you." He was so sweet because he was more concerned about my health than he was about my completing the story.

✧

Abraham was practically flabbergasted one time when he experienced the lengths to which Ashe would go to show a friend that he cared:

On my fortieth birthday, in 1987, we're renting a house in Amagansett on Long Island and my wife is throwing a party for me. Simply as a courtesy we invited Arthur, because he was living with his family in Mount Kisco (New York), and most of the people at the party were friends of mine who had summer homes nearby. Arthur then shows up and says to me, "I just bought a new Volvo station wagon, and I thought it would be fun to take it for a spin." So he drove two and a half hours out to make it for the party and then drove two and a half hours back. Why? Because he thought that would be the right thing, the nice thing, to do. And he says to me, "You know I just did it because I wanted to take my new Volvo out for a ride." A five-hour ride. But that's

Arthur. He would never forget my birthday. Always on my birthday he would send over Le Coq Sportif tennis wear; I'm a tennis player. He always did this. He was very much a man of symbolism, and that kind of stuff was very important to him so that he could let friends know he was thinking of them on their birthday.

~~~

Dell first met Ashe in 1964 as a tennis opponent:

Ironically, the first time I got to know Arthur was in playing him in a tournament at Colonial Country Club in Fort Worth, Texas. He was about twenty-one, and I, being about six or seven years older than Arthur, was getting ready to play my last tournament. I was going back to Washington to practice with a big law firm known as Hogan and Hartson. I graduated from law school in 1964 and played the whole circuit through 1965. I was going back to practicing law and retiring from tennis because in those days there was no prize money, so I wasn't going to keep playing full-time without a job. And you can't be a part-time lawyer when you're with a big firm. I played him in August or September of 1964 and he beat me, pretty easily in fact. He had a big serve, a very whiplash-like serve. I couldn't break his serve on those lightning-fast cement courts.

Arthur was much shyer than most, very reticent. I didn't really get to know Arthur very well until late 1967, when they were trying to talk me into taking the Davis Cup position, and then in early '68 I accepted. Charlie Pasarell, who was his roommate and best friend, as well as a good friend of mine, tried to talk me into taking this job if I was offered it. My first two clients who really changed my life were Arthur Ashe and Stan Smith. And Stan Smith is still a client today.

ꙭ

*Over the years Ashe sometimes took flak for having a white man (Dell) as his lawyer and agent, but their association made perfect sense in **Dell**'s eyes:*

I had an advantage with Arthur I think because I was able to talk with him, I was able to communicate directly with him. I knew his dad who had been a policeman in Richmond. I met his father a few times and for whatever combination of reasons, he liked me, and Arthur's father was everything to him. I was a figurehead to Arthur because I was the captain and he had great respect for whomever was captain, and that was the way he was brought up by his father. I was able to communicate with Arthur and a very intense friendship quickly developed between us. I mean, I represented Arthur for twenty-three years on a handshake and I also represented Michael Jordan for nine years. Arthur was really special and became my best friend during that period.

At Wimbledon in 1975, I was with him the night before at dinner, when we strategized how to beat Connors. It was 16-1 odds with Arthur as the underdog, and he beat Connors in four sets. It was just a lot of relationship there going on between 1968 and 1975, when Arthur ended up being number one in the world. This was a whole group of people that really evolved in the late sixties and seventies through the

Davis Cup team camaraderie that we had created with guys like Jimmy Osborne, Bob Lutz, Stan Smith, and Clark Graebner—they were all damn good friends.

✑

Ashe admitted he had a lot on his mind for most of his life, and it wasn't necessarily any kind of worry that invaded his thoughts and emotions:

I worry sometimes that I'm too open-minded. But then, being open-minded and strongly convicted just can't go hand in hand, can they? And, besides, I have opinions on everything. I'm always thinking. I don't care how tired I am, once I get in bed I can't get to sleep for an hour. There's just so much to think about. Really, I mean it. Ask me about anything and I'll have an opinion right on the tip of my tongue.[1]

✑

*For **Smith** and Ashe, being friends meant being able to deal with mutual aplomb even in an awkward circumstance:*

Arthur and Jeanne's daughter Camera and my daughter Austin liked to play together a lot as they are about the same age. One time all of us were together in a box watching a tennis match, and the girls—who were three or four years old at the time—were playing with two dolls that we had brought for them. Two white dolls. After a while, Arthur said, "I really feel bad about this, because it's not an issue at all, but Camera is playing with a white doll." It wasn't that she shouldn't be playing with a white doll, but the concern was people seeing this and making an issue out of it. So he had the girls get on the ground, out of sight, to play with their dolls. It was an interesting situation but an awkward time.

We were such good friends. I remember one time we were visiting the Ashes at their apartment, and this wasn't long before my son was born. Jeanne, a good photographer, was showing us and Carol Dell, Donald's wife, these photographs she had taken of a labor. They were pretty graphic. It was some sort of project she was doing, and it just so happened that my wife was due three weeks later. Well, that night, she went into labor, on Labor Day. We left the Ashes' apartment about six in the morning to drive out to the hospital. I called Arthur around eight and told him that we were now at the hospital and that it looked like she was going to deliver that day. He asked where we were—he thought we were still in the next bedroom. He didn't even know we were gone.

◈

Added **Smith**:

Arthur and I were godfathers to Donald Dell's twin daughters, so we always had a running competition to see who could be the better godfather.

◈

Rodney Harmon *was about twenty years younger than Ashe, but there was no gap—generation, communication, or otherwise—when it came to understanding what was important about any kind of friendship:*

107

What I remember about him is that he was such an active listener. A lot of people don't appreciate that skill because they are almost always thinking about what they're going to say next. He would listen to what you had to say to completion. He never would rush you or interrupt you, or even give you the impression that he didn't want to hear what you had to say. Now, if it was turning out to be something that was long and drawn-out, he would say, "Hey, you need to give me a call to discuss this more because right now I just don't have the time." One thing about him is that he was always wanting to help people help themselves.

ᕲᗢᗢᕲ

Tom Okker, like most others, saw Ashe as laid back and yet intense in the strength of his beliefs:

Arthur was pretty quiet among the other players. But he was always reading a lot and would express his opinion on a number of things. Still, all things considered, he was pretty quiet. One time he came to my house and I had been collecting art for many years, and, as it turned out, I ended up in the business. He was interested in the art, but then he was interested in a lot of things.

ᕲᗢᗢᕲ

Ashe admitted his dating days as a bachelor showed the fickle side of his nature:

It's not unusual for me to go a month without a date. Of course, wherever I go there are usually Negroes who look me up. But that can be difficult. I try to be nice, but I'm fickle,

I'm choosy no matter what your race happens to be. And however well-meaning these people are I just can't embrace them because we happen to be the only two lumps of coal in the snowbank."[2]

⚬~~∞~~⚬

Dennis Ralston saw Ashe grow wiser in how he treated causes and in how he spoke his mind about issues, and this includes spiritual considerations as well as political:

As he got older and more into the political arena, he was more careful with what he said, and I think that's because he had been coached, but in those days he said whatever he thought. I think he was pretty comfortable with me and respected me, and he was interested in my family. At that time, he was trying to figure out what he believed in. I would be reading the Bible and thinking about how important that was and trying to live that life. He was sort of making fun of it a little bit at the same time he was respecting it, and he respected Stan Smith for his (Christian) beliefs. But Arthur was an agnostic at that time, and I think that changed in his later years, big time, as he got back to his Southern Baptist roots.

⚬~~∞~~⚬

Beck can't forget Ashe's wit, even on mundane matters:

Arthur had a dry sort of wit. When I got a fax machine in 1985, I wrote notes to some of my friends, including Arthur, telling them that I had finally gotten a fax machine and this is my number, and the next thing I know I get a fax back

109

with a short handwritten message on it saying, "Welcome to the 20th century. Arthur."

⁕

Adds **Deford**:

One of the things about Arthur that people have forgotten is what great company he was, what a great sense of humor he had. He's been turned into this legend, which he deserves, but he was also very human and an awful lot of fun.[3]

⁕

Gladys Heldman *discovered another of Ashe's hobbies:*

Arthur liked crossword puzzles, as did I.

⁕

Ashe showed everyone, especially his friends, that how one faces death is as revealing as how one lives his or her own life. **Abraham** *remarks that Ashe had been shouldering the burden of impending death long before he announced in 1992 that he had contracted the AIDS virus:*

I always thought Arthur had very broad shoulders. As he got older he became more world-wise; he traveled more to Africa and other places, and he had more time as he played less tennis. Even before the AIDS was diagnosed, because there was such a history of heart disease in his family, Arthur faced mortality. I'm fifty-three, you're (this book's author) forty-four, and you and I probably don't think that much about death unless we're at a funeral or when somebody's very ill, but thinking about my mortality is not a daily thought. Arthur, because of heart disease in his family— grandfather, father, and uncle—thought about mortality a lot. Arthur confronted it, lived with it, and faced it, and I think that also made him truly world-wise, that that was something he had to live with and that he was in a hurry to do things. I think he lived every day as though it could be his last.

෧᠃ᣉ

Shriver *was among many who got wind of Ashe's possibly having AIDS before he had had a chance to announce it on his own terms:*

There were rumors going around, and as it turned out there were some people close to him who definitely knew. Then it became such a public thing. When it became a public thing everyone felt a little badly because obviously it wasn't done on his own terms. So many times when you have an illness like that you don't want that illness to define you. I knew someone who passed away from cancer and I think, concerning their identity, they want to make sure that while they are struggling to overcome their sickness they don't want that sickness to become something they are known for. Dying from AIDS has to be very similar, except there are even more complicated undercurrents.

I was at a tournament at Amelia Island when I heard about Arthur's death. I had worked with him just several months earlier at a Virginia Slims tournament at Madison

Square Garden and that was when *Sports Illustrated* was putting together a big article on him because he was about to be named *Sports Illustrated*'s Sportsman of the Year. The writer was with him as we were preparing for a telecast, just hanging out and asking questions, just wanting to spend time with Arthur. Then just a few months later, I was coming back from an international trip and found out that he had died and it was like, "Wow."

⚭

Deford was among Ashe's most-trusted few to learn that Ashe had AIDS. Not long after Ashe learned he had contracted the AIDS virus from a transfusion of tainted blood in the early eighties, he contacted Deford to talk about how best to prepare the inevitable public announcement he would someday have to make. As it would turn out, that long-dreaded announcement was forced in 1992 when Ashe learned that USA Today was about the break the story. Years before, after Ashe had learned that he was HIV positive (in 1988), he had tried to contact Deford to break his bad news. Deford at the time was on his way out the door and would be gone for at least a couple of weeks:

I knew he was sick and I wrote him a letter. I was going to Seoul for the Olympics in 1988, and I said I would see him when I got back. I didn't see him immediately when I got back, and I didn't really realize how sick he was until he called me up to tell me. He said, "Look, I've got to tell you something but you've got to promise me that you're not going to tell anybody, to include Carol." And I said, "Oh, Arthur, I can't do that." And he goes, "Well, okay, you can tell Carol, but that's it—she can't tell anyone else and nei-

Just hours before he was to take to the court at Wimbledon for his 1975 singles final against Jimmy Connors, Ashe chilled out while reading the newspaper. (AP/Wide World Photos)

ther can you." I said, "Don't worry," and I didn't have any idea what he was going to say. He said, "When I was in the hospital a few years ago, and I got this blood . . ." And when he said that, I knew what was coming, I don't know how. I was so staggered I don't think I really said anything, but the next time we talked, he talked about how he would need help from me on a statement announcing it. He thought maybe he could keep it a secret for a year or two. The reason he didn't want to bring it out at that time was twofold: Number one, he thought it would be very hard on his daughter, Camera, that people would say things to her; and number two, he knew that once word got out, this was going to define him. He wasn't much worried about people saying things like "Well, you must be gay," and all that kind of

113

thing. All his life he had been, "Arthur Ashe, the first Negro to play tennis," and now he was going to be "Arthur Ashe, AIDS patient." He thought he had about a year or so to live, and in fact it was more like five.

What happened was that the word did get out to some people, but people loved Arthur so much that they kept it a secret. Now I had to keep it a secret, but the people who really deserve credit are the ones who had learned about it without having had to make a promise that they would keep it a secret. They protected him. John Feinstein was one of those. He came to me when we were at *The National* and told me that he had found out. But he said right away, "But don't worry, I would never do anything with it." So all these tough journalists who would die for a scoop, they kept it a secret. It tells you how beloved the guy was that no one wanted to blow the whistle on him. We talked about the statement and that kind of thing, but we always figured that we had time.

I was at the theater in New York that night that USA *Today* called Arthur to ask him to confirm whether or not he had the disease. So I get home from the theater that night and there's a message on my answering machine showing something like eleven o'clock, and he said in the message, "Give me a call." You know, it was typical of Arthur, I wish he had said something more like, "Look, this is what happened, give me a call right away as soon as you get back." It wasn't until the next morning that I called him and found out what the deal was. By then, it was too late. I have since thought that if I could have found out that night, I could have called Gene Policinski (*USA Today*'s sports editor) and said, "Look, here's the deal, Gene. All sorts of journalists have passed on this story, so if you think you're being a real tough, hotshot journalist, don't." Maybe he would have listened to me. By the time I got into the act—and who knows, maybe he would have told me to go to hell—or he could have said, "Well, we do things differently here at *USA Today*." But Arthur was never mad at *USA Today*. He understood that they had to do what they had to do. He had great sympathy for Doug Smith (the newspaper's tennis writer), an old friend of Arthur's, who had walked into this story. They were good friends going back to Virginia, where they knew each other growing up.

The cat's out of the bag by then, but I must give credit to *USA Today* because they refused to go with the story. They still needed more confirmation because Arthur would not admit it, so he had a little time and that's when he decided to prepare the statement and read it. We had known it would come to this someday, but we never knew how it was going to happen. We thought we would have a little more time.

In retrospect, I'm glad that it happened the way it did because, first of all, nothing bad happened. His daughter did not suffer any problems. Even though we didn't know it at the time, he only had about ten months left, but it gave him the opportunity to see just how beloved he was. It was sort of like, it was either Tom Sawyer or Huckleberry Finn—one of them goes to his own funeral. People there think he's dead and he goes back and is standing there listening to all that is being said about him. That's the way it was with Arthur. He read his obituaries before he was dead, and he won all sorts of rewards, too, including *Sports Illustrated*'s Sportsman of the Year and all the stuff that people gave him. It was actually a blessing that it turned out the way it did. I think he had a pretty good last ten months.

I can't remember his being really sick until right at the

end. After he went into the hospital, I went over to see him. I had no idea, and I don't think he did either, that this was the end game. We chatted and spent a long time together. He was planning a Valentine's Day dance, a special dance that was for only fathers and daughters. He had that little daughter. My daughter would have been thirteen, and I was going to bring her. But it wasn't just for fathers and little girls. It was for, say, an eighty-year-old with his fifty-five-year-old daughter. Not even Arthur's own wife, Jeanne, could come. Because it was Valentine's Day, everyone was supposed to wear red and white. The last words I heard from him after I said good-bye and was going out the door was, "Now don't forget to wear red." I'll never forget that. This was like late January.

When I heard about ten days later that Arthur Ashe had died, I said, "No way, no way, Arthur's fine." All I could think was, "Don't forget to wear red." As it turns out, that was the last time I would see him. I never went back to see him again because I had no idea he was as sick as he was, and I don't think he knew either. By then, though, he had lived an awful long time for someone with AIDS. They were still struggling to find out how to deal with it. His being an athlete had to have helped with that. They said the only reason he survived the first heart attack was because he was in such good shape, and he was so skinny. But I guess at the very end he was so worn down that he didn't have any reserves to fight it anymore. Still, he thought he was going to get out of there.

I remember the funeral. It was one of those freakish warm days. It must have been sixty-five degrees in February, in Richmond, and people were lining the streets. We came back to New York for a memorial service two or three days later and it was snowing, an awful day.

◦⟪⟫◦

Beck *was another of Ashe's confidants who carried the knowledge of his condition for more than a year:*

I got to know him well. I was really a confidant of his before it had been leaked that he had AIDS. He only told about a dozen people when he first found out. I am honored to be able to call him a friend. It was probably the biggest personal burden I've ever felt, because at various tennis meetings and national conferences, a few people were starting to think there might be something wrong. People knew that I knew him well and they would ask me if he was sick, and, of course, I had to lie and I'm not very good at that. Somebody mentioned that they heard he had AIDS, and I was so distressed by that question that I called Arthur and told him this person had suggested to me they thought you might have AIDS and that I had tried to dodge it and deny it. He said, "I know. Word is starting to get out a little bit."

⌒⫘⌒

Harmon *recalls the last time he spoke with Ashe, which wasn't long before Ashe passed away:*

We talked about a week before he died. I remember him coughing a lot, and this was when I had called him to ask his opinion about something we were doing at the USTA related to some of the up-and-coming minority players. In talking to him, I said, "Gosh, you sound really bad, you need to take it easy," and he said, "I feel okay, I'm just not doing so well right now. I've got so many things to do I just can't afford to rest." I then went out to Vancouver where I was taking some kids for a tournament. I was sitting in the stands watching some of the matches and someone had a little TV with them watching the news, and then news came across that he had died. So I called the USTA and they sent another coach out to replace me and I went to Richmond for the funeral.

One of my favorite stories concerns about his love to talk about education. He cared especially about having good writing skills. He liked to write and was very much into writing and writing clearly. One time after a clinic at Doral I told him, "You know, Arthur, you really spend a lot of time with these kids. I'm sure they appreciate it." And what he said to me was, "Well, one of the interesting things about that is that when you do something for someone else, you bring more joy to yourself than anything else you do. It really means a lot to me helping other people."

༺∞༻

Stan Smith *also spoke with Ashe not long before his death:*

I talked to him about a week or so before he died. I think he felt he was on the way to recovery—that he was going to beat it. One fellow that my wife and I had gotten to know pretty well thought that he had a serum that could help cure the HIV and AIDS. We spent a lot of time with this guy. The bottom line, however, is that Arthur's doctor felt he was taking so much medication already that he couldn't take any more. So, who knows what would have happened had he been able to do it? The ironic thing about it is that years earlier I would be taking Vitamin C and a few other supplements, and he would ask me why I'm taking all those pills. And I would say, "Oh, there might be something in here that might prevent a cold or the flu or that sort of thing," and he said, "I've never taken a pill before in my life." This was before he had the problems with his leg and then with his heart. Ironically, he ended up taking so much medication that it was mind-boggling. He felt that his medication, the AZT I guess it was, was making him better. He was feeling better.

There were terrible things that he went through—having to go to the bathroom so much, the sores around his mouth, and difficulty in eating. But he never complained about his fate. This attitude goes back to when he wasn't allowed to play in a club, or he wasn't able to go into a particular tournament, or he wasn't able to go into their clubhouse. Arthur wouldn't dwell on the issue. Then he had the heart problems and the AIDS, and he didn't dwell on those things either. He thought he was going to beat it.

I found out about Arthur's death while I was playing in the AT&T golf tournament, partnered with (golf pro) John Inman. We had just made the cut and Saturday night we were at a restaurant, and somebody came in and said that Arthur had died. It was a shock.

⌒⌒⌒

Eisenberg has one deep regret that goes beyond Ashe's death itself:

One of the biggest holes in my life was missing his memorial service. I've never been able to put closure to this. I was on my way trying to get there (New York), and there was a snowstorm and I was sitting in the airport when it was announced that all flights had been canceled and you couldn't get to New

York (from Philly). So I ran to another side of the airport. I was in tears because I really felt like I needed to be there. Charlie Pasarell was waiting and he told me to stay back where I was because he really believed we could still get on some other flight scheduled to go to New York, but I didn't believe him.

As it turned out, I never made it there and Charlie did, and I was told that he gave one of the inspiring talks at the service. Chris Beck knows how upset I was and I kept calling her to see if I could still get there, but she told me it was almost over. To this day when someone brings Arthur's name up I can't get past that. It was so important that I be there for myself as much as for him.

⌒∞⌒

Abraham remembers exactly where he was and what he was doing when he received word of Ashe's death:

This is really easy, and very sad. I don't have to search at all. The night he died, HBO did a prize fight at Madison Square Garden. It was Riddick Bowe, the heavyweight champion, fighting Michael Dokes. Arthur was going to go with me to the fight that night as he was a very avid prize fight fan and very knowledgeable. Over the years he probably went to a half-dozen prize fights with me as his schedule permitted, and since the fight was in New York I invited him. He went into the hospital, either that Thursday or Friday, with pneumonia—his lungs were filling up with fluid. So I took somebody else. Around eight o'clock, just as the main event was getting ready to start, one of HBO's security people found me, leaned over, and said, "Arthur just died." I just totally drew a blank. It took me sixty seconds to grasp it. Then I got somebody in our truck and we made an announcement over the air during the live telecast that Arthur had died. They tolled the bell at Madison Square Garden ten times out of respect for him, when traditionally they do for people in the fight community. But because Arthur was bigger than the fight community as well as a big prize fight fan, they tolled the bell. It was a painful memory, but easy to recall.

❧

*Said **Dell***:

America lost a great deal when Arthur passed away and it was much more than just tennis.

❧

5

CITIZEN OF THE WORLD

Muhammad Ali probably was the world's most-recognized sports celebrity during the late sixties and through the seventies, and Ashe wasn't far behind in that same era. Like Ali, Ashe had global appeal because his notoriety transcended his sport. But other than being black, a champion in his sport, and having a last name that began with an A, Ali and Ashe had little else in common. While both were citizens of the world, Ashe was a serious student of international politics and respected worldwide for his quiet dignity in dealing with potentially explosive issues.

Ashe's international political activism didn't begin and end with his 1973 trip to South Africa. In 1985, the same year he was voted into the International Tennis Hall of Fame, he was arrested in Washington, D.C., while protesting apartheid outside the South African embassy. Then in 1991, Ashe joined a delegation of thirty other well-known African

Americans in traveling to South Africa to be a witness to political changes that were underway there involving the integration of blacks and whites. A year later Ashe was again arrested in Washington, D.C., this time for protesting U.S. treatment of refugees from Haiti. Three months later, on World AIDS Day, Ashe spoke to the United Nations General Assembly, beseeching U.N. delegates to raise funds for AIDS research.

Appropriately symbolic of Ashe's involvement in politics as well as his many travels around the world as an ambassador of tennis was a T-shirt he often wore that said "Citizen of the World." Before going on his international trips, Ashe was known to read up on whatever his destination was to be, both in terms of being a tourist and so he could better understand the culture and language of the country. One of his trips overseas during the height of the Vietnam War took him to Vietnam, where he visited a hospital housing badly wounded American soldiers. One of the soldiers, who apparently didn't know who Ashe was, looked at the tennis star and said he figured Ashe was somebody well known because he recognized him from pictures he had seen. Yes, Ashe got around.

❧

Stan Smith traveled extensively outside the United States with Ashe, whether it was to compete in international tournaments or take part in exhibition tours in which they were the main attractions. This gave Smith ample opportunity to see how the rest of the world regarded Ashe, and vice versa.

No matter where Arthur played outside the United States,

people looked at him differently than they looked at me. Obviously, for one thing, he was black. They were kind of curious of what black athletes were like, and I think they were more receptive in some ways to American black athletes and that's why Arthur was a tremendous ambassador on behalf of the United States. One of his favorite T-shirts said "Citizen of the World." That basically stood for what he believed in—that the world was a small place and we all have to live together. He was very proud to be an American, but he also felt that in all his travels around the world that the world was one place and not just one made up of different factions or countries. I thought that was kind of significant.

Another interesting tour for us was when we went to Africa, and this is a favorite story of mine I have told a number of times. I was the number one–ranked player at the time accompanying Arthur, who I think was number three at the time. This was around 1970 or 1971. It was just the two of us traveling all over with three reporters with us—Frank Deford, Richard Evans, and Bud Collins. They were covering his involvement in Africa, and obviously the trip revolved around Arthur. We went around the country playing these matches against each other. It was sort of like Arthur was the Harlem Globetrotters and I was the Washington Generals, supposedly the designated other guy as everyone thronged around Arthur. We would be playing in these exhibitions and the announcers would introduce him as "Arthur Ashe, the number-one player in the United States yada, yada, yada," and then it would be my turn and they would go, "And Stan Smith, his opponent." After this went on about five or six times, I finally had had about enough and mentioned it to these three reporters with us, saying something to the effect that, "This is getting on my nerves a little bit." Well, Arthur got wind of this, and next time I saw him, he came up to me and said, "Tell you what, when we do our trip to Alabama, I'll carry your racket around for you."

⚭

Ashe wasn't just a world-traveling ambassador of tennis, he also was a role model whose charisma and attitudes reflected ideals that crossed cultural and political boundaries, as **Pam Shriver** *points out:*

Color had something to do with it, but so did his personality and the fact that he had a lot of things to say from a social aspect, such as the whole thing about his trip to South Africa. He was just sort of a lightning rod for discussion about things. Arthur always had something to say about things going on in the world and that made him stand out, a little like the way Billie Jean King stands out or maybe Martina Navratilova—people who are willing to talk about more things than just their sport. They transcend the sport. The fact that Arthur was black made him even more of an original. He was raised in such a way as to be a bridge between groups of people. There aren't many people who can bridge different groups such as races or religions, but he was able to do that.

In 1978, with Arthur Ashe on the men's side and Billie Jean King on the women's side, you had pretty good examples of role models who could make younger people realize that they could have a greater role in society or that they could branch out. And in order to be really effective, you have to be a champion, and both of them certainly were that. Arthur won Wimbledon and the U.S. Open, and while he never got to be number one in the world, he certainly was a champion; and Billie Jean King was not only a great person for representing causes but one of the great champions in the game. That's a very powerful combination. I had a little bit of success in the singles and the doubles, but nowhere near what they accomplished. Being a champion is something that not enough athletes take advantage of. There are areas in which people like Arthur and Billie Jean can make a difference, and people will listen. Another good example is baseball player Mark McGwire when it comes to talking out about child abuse. I think Michael Jordan is an example of someone who didn't necessarily want to embrace any cultural or social issue, even though he's a model citizen. I think Arthur really helped a lot of things along.

⟨✦⟩

When Ashe went abroad, he usually was accompanied by several reporters, one of whom, **Bud Collins,** *thought it commendable that Ashe and his peers would voluntarily go on State Department trips, even when there wasn't a huge paycheck waiting for them on the other end:*

One of the great things about Arthur which you would never find people doing today is making these State Department tours. It was very important to him. He made one in 1970 to Africa and another one there in 1971. Then he went to South Africa in 1973 and then there was the Southeast Asia Tour. Guys like him and Stan Smith were glad to do that for their country. I don't even know if such things even exist anymore. He and Stan Smith played all the matches during one of the Africa trips. It was them, Frank Deford, Richard Evans, and me—the five of us—visiting Kenya, Tanzania, Uganda, Zambia, Nigeria, and Ghana. Those were difficult in some respects, such as in Tanzania, which was a Socialist country leaning very much toward China, which was not good in the official U.S. view in those days. They had had an American singing group there, Up With People, and they had been heckled. People threw things at them, driving them off the stage. It had been a very anti-American display. The ambassador said to us, "Now look, when you go out to the tennis court, there are going to be people like that there, and it's going to be the same sort of situation. And if anything starts, you will need to leave. We're not trying to provoke anybody. So we'll just go." Well, Stan and Arthur went out there in their USA jackets and the people were receptive. Sports seems to have a little bit of an in with people. The people were delighted and it was a big hit, and that's the way it turned out to be everywhere. But Tanzania was the one place people had been worried about. It worked out very, very well.

When we were in Zambia, which I think was the fourth stop, we were sitting around having a beer—Stan Smith was the highest-ranked player at the time, yet everywhere we went Arthur was introduced as the world champion playing "another American," Stan Smith—and when we got to the airport we were met by a television reporter, a man named Charlie Yo-Yo, I'll never forget that. He was seated between Arthur and Stan, and all he wanted to do was interview Arthur. So he turned in such a way that his back was to Stan the entire interview. And then after he had had about five or ten minutes with Arthur, he finally turned around to Stan and asked, "Mr. Smith, how do you like our country?" and

Stan said something like "It's fine." and that was the end of the interview. Stan was steaming a little.

So then we were in this bar and this was the only time I ever heard Stan Smith swear. And he said, "Jesus Christ, Arthur, I mean, you're like God here, and they don't even recognize that I'm here," and that's when Frank Deford said, "You don't get it, Stan, do you? Have you looked around at the people? You know, they're kind of a different color, and you are the big O." And Stan goes, "What do you mean by that?" Frank says, "You are the *opponent*. Joe Louis used to have a Bum of the Month Club, and that's who you are." Stan chuckled at that. And that's the way it was everywhere we went.

⌒⟋⟋⟍⟍⌒

*Another way of classifying Ashe was as a statesman, a description that friend **Seth Abraham** used in comparing Ashe to another notable American:*

Thomas Jefferson is buried in a family cemetery on the grounds of Monticello, his estate in Monticello, Virginia. It's in northwest Virginia and I've been there twice. He's buried in a family plot on the grounds of the estate, and on his tombstone, which he wrote, it makes no mention that he was a president of the United States. When he died, of course, there had been only five or six presidents at the time, but still no mention. It does mention that he was a founder of the University of Virginia, that he was one of the writers of the Declaration of Independence, and I think it says "statesman-diplomat," because he was an ambassador to France. So here's a man who was arguably the greatest president in our nation's history, and certainly in the top five, but what he valued was not necessarily being president. For Arthur, there is a monument to his life in Richmond on the Avenue of Heroes in which he is carrying schoolbooks and he has an arm around children, and books were a very important part of Arthur's life. His epitaph in Virginia—he's buried in Richmond—has tennis listed last: Author, father, husband, citizen, humanitarian—but his tennis accomplishment is really downplayed; he's not buried as a tennis star, he's buried as a citizen.

◦⁓⁓⁓๑

Before he gave up tennis to become a full-time attorney and subsequently the founder of Pro-Serve, **Donald Dell** *hung out with Ashe and his tennis-playing contemporaries, allowing him to get to know them well. Dell had been a topnotch player himself. By the time he was eighteen, he had won two boys national championships and beaten Rod Laver twice, although by the time Dell had graduated from Yale, Laver had skyrocketed to number one in the world. Dell recalls those days with fondness:*

Remember, I was living and traveling and dating with those guys. I was the youngest captain and I was single, and while they were all six or seven years younger than me, they were contemporaries when I stopped playing, so I knew them pretty well. They were all better players than I was.

Because I was traveling, I spent a lot of time with these guys. We made it a real big mission when it came to Davis Cup play, and the six guys really made the commitment. There was no big conflicting prize money in those days. Arthur and Charlie Pasarell were both still in the service, so I had the travel orders for them and they would travel with the team. I had good leverage with them because they would rather be traveling with the Davis Cup team than to be stationed at Fort Ord or wherever. That was a tremendous advantage for me and the team. We built esprit de corps and a good team attitude, and my goal when I picked Dennis Ralston as our coach to replace Pancho Gonzalez (very gently and quietly—I let him resign—but I wasn't going to repeat with him) was to win, period. We had great training. We trained for two weeks before every match, and my goal was to emulate Vince Lombardi and make practice sessions so difficult that the matches would seem easier by comparison. We had two-a-days and five-set challenge matches as we worked their tails off that first week—and then slowed it down for the second week, then we had the draw on Thursday and the first match on Friday.

I always believed that preparation was the whole ballgame, and if we were in best shape and really prepared, then we would have the best team. We beat Australia in the finals and earned our way into the challenge round for 1969, at which time we played in the finals against Romania, which had Ian Tiriac and Ilie Nastase. That was a very tough match. The first three or four of the five matches were extended, but we went on to win.

☙❧

Ashe knew that when he went to South Africa in 1973 he was doing much more than getting ready to play in a tennis tournament:

I don't think I can visit this country without it having political ramifications.[1]

☙❧

Ashe focuses in as he goes to the net. (AP/Wide World Photos)

*One of the finest lessons in life that Ashe ever passed on to his Richmond protege **Rodney Harmon** was to take a look at the world around you as you traveled the globe, always ready to soak in the sights and sounds, and language if need be. Harmon reminisces:*

Arthur used to carry Berlitz tapes around with him all the time because he was trying to become fluent in Spanish and French.

When I was getting ready to go to England, he told me to make sure that I took the time to get out to see things and to see all the things that London has. "Get out to the Tower of London and go to see Westminster Abbey," Arthur said.

He would always sightsee and learn about the local history, and he wanted me to share in that kind of an experience, too.

❧

Ashe was also ahead of his time in the area of equal opportunities for both genders, as **Pam Shriver** *found out more than twenty years ago, which she explains in a nice little vignette:*

Probably my clearest memory of Arthur dates back to my early playing days. I started out in professional tennis in 1978, about when he was in the last couple years of his career. In his last big singles final, Arthur was playing McEnroe in the Masters at Madison Square Garden. It could have been in 1978 or 1979; I'm not quite clear on that. Anyway, I had been asked to come up there and play in an exhibition match on the day of the finals, a mixed-doubles match because I think they had only that singles match and wanted another match to go with it. Arthur was going to play his singles match against John McEnroe in the afternoon. I was warming up for my mixed-doubles match with my coaches earlier when Arthur walks into the practice area. He had nobody to hit with, so he asked me if I would hit with him. I said, "Sure," so I warmed him up for his match. And what's so interesting about that is that there are so few guys who would do something like that—let a women player hit with him for a warm-up. There's no reason why not, but that shows you how open Arthur's mind was about things. There's no reason I couldn't warm him up for twenty minutes or whatever. What I remember about hitting it with him is that his key weapons were a really good first serve. He played a really aggressive game in coming to the net and was difficult to pass, but it wasn't like I had the opportunity to watch him play that many matches.

❧

No discussion of Ashe and all that he contributed to the world beyond tennis can avoid the phrase "transcended the game," as fellow tennis player **Eliot Teltscher** *explains:*

He transcended the game, and there aren't a lot of players that I feel really transcended the game. Ask me to name somebody else and I can't come up with another name that quickly. There have been a lot of great players, but he changed the game, he really did. Other sports have had more athletes transcend their respective games but tennis hasn't had much of that. Up until the last few years, with the Williams sisters (Venus and Serena) starting to change things a little bit, players have pretty much been cookie-cutter. It seems like they have pretty much been coming from the same place wearing the same clothes and pretty much playing the same game. It's kind of a small group of people when you think about today's players, whereas Arthur clearly transcended the game. No question about it. Maybe you could put Billie Jean King into that same category, too, in part because of the Bobby Riggs thing and what she did for women's tennis. But as great tennis players as Jimmy Connors and Chris Evert were, and they both are good people as well, they really don't go beyond the game. In that respect, Arthur and Billie Jean would go into a different category.

❧

Among the many things that former World Tennis Magazine *publisher* **Gladys Heldman** *admired about Ashe was the gracious manner in which he handled triumph as well as prejudice:*

First of all he won Wimbledon, which is something very few people ever do. Secondly, he always handled himself so well with everything. He was a standout from those times when he didn't even know if a tournament would accept his entry. It was difficult. This was a big time of big prejudices by many people, particularly at the private tennis clubs, although not in the major indoor arenas where there were no problems. The first one who had to face this was Althea Gibson, and she handled herself beautifully, too. Occasionally, she would make a mistake like when she lost to Doris Hart in the finals of what I think was the National Clay Courts, when she said to Doris, "Next time I'll beat you," and Doris got quite mad and said, "Do you want to play for money right now?" It was because Althea did not know the tradition, one of which is that you don't say, "Next time I'll beat you." You say, in a Japanese style way, "You were too good and I tried my best, but you were too good." If you win, you say, "I was lucky." Arthur very, very seldom made a mistake like this and if he did, I don't know what it was.

Arthur got more poised as he got older. When Owen Williams, who ran tennis for South Africa, invited Arthur to come play tennis in South Africa, he had to pull some strings with the government to allow Arthur to come in. Arthur could have said yes or he could have said no, but he said yes, even though one group of blacks criticized him for that. Well, Arthur helped to break the barriers in South Africa because suddenly, when he played, they had to allow blacks in the gallery.

⌒〜〜〜⌒

Christine Beck saw time and time again the selfless side of Ashe, who went out of his way to make the youngsters to whom he gave clinics feel comfortable and valued:

This man was so amazing—the commitments he honored beyond what a normal person would do. It was incredible. Let me give you two examples. One was five days after this news broke that he had AIDS, he was scheduled to come to Philadelphia for our benefit and a kids clinic at the Arthur Ashe Youth Tennis Center. Some people would have rethought that, but not Arthur. He came. The kids were so wonderful and he was so wonderful, even with the press all over the place making things crazier than ever. He handled it with such confidence, aplomb, and peace. The other time was less than two weeks before he died. He was scheduled to tape a video for us at the youth center here. It was scheduled for a studio in New York City, and our press person went up there—and I think I was out of town and to this day I totally regret not making the effort to go that day—but he went ahead and took about an hour and a half to tape a video for us, so we have this very special piece of him talking about this center here in Philadelphia and the good work it's doing and how important it was to him having an indoor center like this for kids. He does look sick in the video, but he does smile and his eyes twinkle.

He wanted to continue to have the opportunity for as

long as he could to live the life that he wanted to and to make his choices without being pulled into AIDS issues, and I have to respect that. One time he remarked how he had been on the front pages of sports sections of newspapers before and now here he was on the front page of the paper, period. He accomplished a great deal; his life was too short.

෴

Smith said that sometimes the challenge of keeping up with Ashe went beyond the tennis court as well, such as when it came time to speak the native language of whatever country they might be playing in at a given time. A little preparation never hurt:

I can't remember exactly when Arthur and I first met, but we became very good friends through tennis. We were also in a business together and got to hang out a lot away from the court while we were playing Davis Cup competition around the world. We also did several tours together, going to places such as France, Africa, and Asia. There are certain things that occurred during those tours that remain pretty memorable, such as the time that Arthur and I were playing each other during the France tour. In fact, there was a time when we actually ended up playing each other in the finals of a tournament held in Paris. At the time there was also a popular program in France that was kind of a funny wrap-up show that they had.

They had Arthur and me on this show one time, and you've got to realize that we were expected to know at least a little French. They would ask each of us a question in French and we had to give the answer in French. At least they gave us a little bit of advance notice of what they were going to ask so that we would be able to think of what we were going to say in response. To get ready, we both went through some answers with each other. Now, Arthur actually had taken some French and he actually had become pretty good in translating and speaking. For one particular question he asked, "How do you say player?" or something like that, and then he went on the show and gave the answer. After that week, people would come up to us around France as we were touring and say, "You speak French so well." It really made a big dent in terms of establishing our reputation in France of both. We weren't very good at conversing in French, but when we tried to say something in French, people there thought we could at least speak French a little, and that was good enough. When we went to dinners over there, Arthur would get up and speak a little bit of French, and of course, that was a big hit as well. He was pretty conversant in it eventually. By the way, my tennis shoe was made in France, and it still is actually, but it helped me from a public-relations standpoint.

༾

Ashe was meticulous in preparation for everything he did, whether it was giving speeches, putting on clinics, plotting out strategy for his next tennis match, dressing himself, speaking at least a little French, or working to improve his skills as a television tennis commentator. HBO Sports's **Abraham** *saw Ashe's* *due diligence up close during the eighties as Ashe went the extra mile to improve his commentating talents:*

There are very few men or women who are naturals, who get it the first time you put a microphone in their hands. You're not born with a microphone in your hands and talking to millions of people while looking at the camera and trying to pretend that the camera is another person. Arthur, like everybody else as a broadcaster, grew into it and over the years really worked at it. He didn't just phone it in, as in go to Wimbledon, spend two weeks, then go home. He wanted to know if he was getting better and what he could do to get better. He spent time working in the studio and he read everything he could read about tennis after he had been off the tour so that he could pronounce names correctly. In tennis, where you have so many Europeans, so many eastern Europeans now, even Russians, all with polysyllabic names, he was always concerned about pronouncing a player's name right, both as a courtesy to the player and because he wanted to get it right for the viewer. He rarely fumbled on a name because he would rehearse it, repeat it over and over in his mind to make sure he got it right. Of course, he got better, became more polished, and he always knew the inner game. And that's nothing to take for granted because knowing it and then being able to communicate it to other people is different. That's not Arthur sitting around in a group with other tennis players talking about it; it's Arthur talking to twenty-eight million HBO subscribers and communicating it to them.

⊙━━━⊙

Ashe certainly was looking up as he defeated Tom Okker to win the men's singles title at the inaugural U.S. Open, held in 1968. (AP/Wide World Photos)

Getting back to the overseas trips, **Smith** *remembers one in particular in which they spent some time in Vietnam during the height of the Vietnam War:*

One trip I'll never forget was our second tour of Asia, when we went from Hawaii to Alaska and on to Tokyo, eventually making it into Vietnam. What made this trip kind of strange was that it came during the holiday season and we actually missed experiencing Christmas day. Here's how it happened: On the twenty-fourth of December, we flew out of Anchorage and got to Tokyo quite late on the twenty-fifth, and in Tokyo there's very little sign of Christmas. So there we were, the two of us, missing the whole day of Christmas because of the length of our trip and how time zones are arranged. That was kind of an odd time.

We went to Vietnam twice. In those days he was either in the army or just getting out of the service. I'm not sure. I wasn't in the service at the time myself, although I did join up several years later. One of the times when we were in Vietnam it was New Year's Eve and the other time it was in early January 1970, I believe. If I remember right, these were state department tours where we went and visited the American troops and played some exhibition matches in Vietnam. One time I remember in particular was when we played at the Cirque Sortif, which was the main tennis club in Saigon and which had been started by the French. Some of the American military leaders were there to watch us play, as were representatives from the (South) Vietnamese military. There were also several hundred soldiers there, and you've got to keep in mind that this was right in the

141

middle of a war going on. The joke was that if you went to hit the ball and saw two of them, you could bet that one was a hand grenade and that it was time to run for cover. Certainly Arthur was a big hit with the soldiers, especially at different hospitals, both black and white soldiers. This was yet another one of those things where he would give of his time—that's the story of his life.

⁂

Bud Collins elaborates on the trip to Vietnam:

The Americans went to Australia at the end of 1968 to play the Davis Cup, and I think it was mainly through Arthur's urging that the team made a goodwill tour in January, a State Department goodwill tour, of Southeast Asia, which would include Vietnam. I think he felt he wanted to at least present his body in Vietnam. I was with him on that trip. We went to Indonesia, Thailand, Burma—which was very unusual because no one ever got into Burma. Charlie Pasarell was with us. We had a clinic with some young kids, including two of the children of the dictator at the time. Charlie had a stock speech whenever they did this kind of thing, saying, "You kids are going to have to practice hard, and you've got to travel because tennis is a game where you have to travel to find the competition, that it's not like staying in your hometown and playing high school basketball. You've really got to move around." Finally, Arthur nudged Charlie and said, "For God's sake, Charlie, these people can't get out of this country. What are you talking about?"

We also went to Laos. Arthur missed a couple days of this because he had to fly back to New York to accept some kind of award that the army was giving him. But he was back in time for when we went through Vietnam, a trip segment that lasted about a week. They played exhibitions in Vietnam at places like Da Nang and Saigon. On the day we played in Saigon, all the top brass from the South Vietnamese military and the U.S. military were there to watch. While we were there, we got a report that because of all the people being there at once, the Viet Cong had targeted the place. So we were all a little shaky. The first time we heard some artillery going off, all the players hit the deck on the court and the soldiers were all laughing, saying, "That's outgoing artillery, fellows. You've got to learn to distinguish between the outgoing and the incoming." But it was pretty loud.

Anyway, they were all lined up to play, but no one was really that anxious to play because of that report about the Viet Cong targeting the place. Fortunately nothing happened. I do remember we had a major, Willis Johnson, who was in charge of our group. When we arrived at the airport, Arthur had a sort of semi-Afro and Pasarell, who was in the air force, had hair that was down fairly long at the time. Major Johnson greets us and then tells Arthur and Charlie, "Okay, fellows, the first thing you're going to do is get a haircut and wear your uniform."

I remember it being hot as hell. Driving from the airport we were in this car with all the windows rolled up, and so Pasarell rolls down a window. And Major Johnson says, "Roll that window up, Pasarell. Tell you what, you leave a window down and sometimes a little guy will ride by on a bike and drop a grenade in your lap." And Pasarell rolled up the window very quickly.

We got to a very nice club, an old French Club where Major Johnson said, "Collins, you'll umpire." And I said, "Really?" So I got up there in the umpire's chair and it seemed higher than any other umpire's chair I had ever seen. After I got up there, I said, "Gee, I feel like a pretty good target up here," and he said, "That's right, and that's why you're up high and I'm not." So I was up there calling all the lines and I gave the Americans every break because I wanted to get it over with quickly. The U.S. was playing against the South Vietnamese Davis Cup team. We didn't realize they had a team, but it was another U.S. taxpayer-supported endeavor. They could only play road matches in Davis Cup play then, though, because no one could come to Saigon.

All in all, it was a great trip. The tough part about it was visiting the hospitals, for Arthur and Charlie to see guys their age or younger who were going to be in hospitals for the rest of their lives. Some wouldn't want to talk but others would make the effort. Some were just glad to see the American guys. None of them really knew much about tennis, but one guy, when he saw Arthur, said, "You're somebody, aren't you? I've seen your picture somewhere," and they got to talking. I think it made Arthur feel a little better about his situation because now he had made some sort of effort.

☙

Being a citizen of the world was a responsibility that Ashe gladly took on—at times, anyway:

Marching in a protest is a liberating experience. It's cathartic. It's one of the great moments you can have in your life.[2]

~~~

Collins knew Ashe as punctual and reliable, but there was an occasional higher calling that would sometimes take precedence over protocol:

I don't remember the last time I saw Arthur, but I do remember one time when we were both supposed to be on the

In 1992 Ashe took part in a demonstration outside the White House protesting President George Bush's policy on Haiti. Ashe was among those arrested. (Greg Gibson, AP/Wide World Photos)

145

Charlie Rose show. But he didn't show up, nor did he phone, and this was so uncharacteristic of him. We were worried because we knew he had been ill and that he had had heart attacks. But it turns out he had been arrested that day protesting the treatment of Haitians. This might have been 1991. He was a peaceful demonstrator.

ᏇᏇᎧ

Whenever Ashe came to Philadelphia, **Chris Beck** *would be there to meet him and would never fail to be impressed with his concern for other people—those he knew and loved, as well as those he had never met:*

Whenever he came to town, I would pick him up either at the airport or train station and we would always eat a meal before the first interview or whatever was scheduled during his visit. One of the events was taking place at the mayor's reception room in city hall. We were walking through city hall and he was always being recognized by people, especially African Americans, and this one time there was a prisoner in handcuffs being led down this big dreary hall and he recognized Arthur and it was a "Hi, brother, keep the faith" kind of thing. Arthur was just so real, and he cared, about his family above all. He absolutely adored Jeanne and Camera. One time he had left home too early for him to say good-bye to his little girl and he called her from the car in Philadelphia so that he could be able to say good morning to her. That was very important to him.

ᏇᏇᎧ

In this tribute to Ashe, Sports Illustrated *writer* **Kenny Moore** *placed Ashe into some pretty fast company in terms of sports history:*

In sporting deportment, Ashe was a contemporary of Joe DiMaggio, just barely tipping his cap to acknowledge the crowd after a home run, or of Jim Brown, calmly handing the ball to the official in the end zone, a trail of writhing would-be tacklers sufficient testimony to his work well done. Ashe was of a time when the core of the American athlete was a sense of fair play. He believed he had control of his own behavior and therefore responsibility for his character.[3]

⚬⚬⚬⚬

Dennis Ralston*'s appreciation of Ashe extended into how well Ashe handled himself as Davis Cup captain dealing with the likes of John McEnroe and Jimmy Connors as team members:*

Arthur got Rodney Harmon to come to SMU and he looked out for Rodney. I think Arthur by this time (early eighties) was just starting to get into all that other stuff taking over his life in later years, such as the ATP and being a national fig-ure. His winning Wimbledon (in 1975) launched him into another level. Then he became Davis Cup captain and had his run-ins with (Jimmy) Connors just like we all did and he handled it with dignity. (John) McEnroe, too. To me, that was the ultimate test for Arthur. I would have thrown McEnroe off the team and said that we could do without him. Then again, Arthur may have liked the challenge of trying to be able to work with McEnroe. His ability to work with John fell somewhere in between failure and success.

McEnroe every now and then said nice things about Arthur, so he made a good impression, but I don't think he changed the way that McEnroe played.

∽⌾∽

Legendary tennis coach **Nick Bollettieri** *summed up Ashe this way:*

Everything he did he did it basically in the same way—very honestly and with a certain flamboyance in his mannerisms.

∽⌾∽

6

THE LEGACY

Ashe passed away on February 6, 1993, eight days shy of a special Valentine's Day dance for fathers and daughters that he had been planning in previous weeks. Even his closest friends were surprised to learn of Ashe's death from AIDS-related pneumonia, because just a week or so earlier he had seemed better with an optimistic prognosis. But that's the curse of AIDS, which can take otherwise healthy individuals and break them down either bit by bit or in one fell swoop.

The legacy Ashe left behind is evident in many ways. He was the first African-American male to break into big-time tennis and win Grand Slam events, which is roughly the equivalent of what Tiger Woods has been doing in golf in recent years. Ashe was also an active leader in finding funding and making opportunities for more youngsters to have unprecedented access to tennis facilities and instruction. As an activist, he campaigned for the abolishment of apartheid in South Africa, among other causes. He was a role model for African Americans, yet never a yes man when it came to endorsing policies and courses of actions recommended by other black leaders. Ashe was a living model of Teddy Roosevelt's motto of "Speaking softly and carrying a big stick," whether the subject be heart disease, AIDS research, or education.

Ashe's legacy is not only measured by the tennis trophies he won, and they are many, but also by the tennis centers and foundation named after him, as well as the educational programs he helped start. Ashe was also the embodiment of sportsmanship, his reputation was firmly established as an athlete who adhered to rules of competition as well as etiquette. In defeat, he was gracious; in victory he was humble. If Ashe didn't have a flair for the outrageous, he certainly had a flair for outstanding citizenship and sportsmanship.

Three months before he passed away, Ashe was named *Sports Illustrated*'s Sportsman of the Year. After his death, statues commemorating him and the life he lived were erected outside the new Forest Hills tennis stadium named after him, and on Richmond's Monument Avenue alongside monuments dedicated to Confederate heroes. Even now, Ashe's legacy transcends statues and trophies.

 ⌒〰〰♀

Nick Bollettieri *says that Ashe's legacy is multifaceted and that tennis was not only just a part of the equation, but it may not even have been the biggest part:*

Most tennis players are one-dimensional: that's their life. But everything that Arthur did and touched and spoke, he did it from the standpoint of being much more than just a tennis player. If you didn't get to see him play tennis, you might not have believed that he was a tennis player. That's what made Arthur such a great person. He was so quiet, but very deliberate when he spoke. He could be very forceful without being demanding. He wasn't the type who would say, "You've gotta do this" or "You've gotta do that." He would start off by saying, "What are we going to do?" That's one thing that made him so interesting.

He opened the doors and made people very conscious of the need to help blacks, but he didn't bang it to death. All of the really great qualities of Arthur didn't surface until he got sick. He wasn't a high-flyer generating all that publicity like an Agassi or a McEnroe. To me, his greatness on and off the tennis court didn't really surface until right before he passed away—how he handled that situation while he was still living was something wonderful.

⌒≈≈≈⌒

Journalist **Bud Collins** *points to a contemporary tennis superstar in making a comparison that aptly describes Ashe's greatness:*

A great legacy is something that Pete Sampras has defined very well, and that is that you can be a great champion and be a sportsman at the same time. People today think you've got to be outrageous for the most part, in your face and in your attitude, stuff like that. I do remember one time that Arthur did lose his temper and hit the ball into the stands. It was in Denver, in 1974, and I forgot who he was playing, and I said, "That's an automatic fine," and Mike Davies, who was in charge of WCT at that time, said, "That's the hardest fine that I've ever had to levy." I mean, can you imagine actually *fining* Arthur Ashe for unsportsmanlike conduct?

Speaking of sportsmanship, I also remember the Masters held in Stockholm in 1975. In one round-robin match it was Arthur against Ilie Nastase, who's the reason for the code of conduct because he got away with so much stuff. Arthur was beating him, and Nastase was stalling, arguing, everything. Finally, Arthur just threw up his hands and said, "That's it," and he just walked out, automatically defaulting. Everyone was shocked because he was winning the match. Everybody was dismayed because obviously Nastase was the culprit. The referee, a guy from Germany, went into the dressing room to plead with Arthur to return. "Please come back. You're not at fault." And Arthur said, "I refuse. I walked and so therefore I defaulted. I quit." He was a man of principles. Everyone there watching was confused by the whole thing because there had been no announcement of who the winner was. When it was clear that Arthur was not going to return, the referee said "I am defaulting Nastase because it was in my mind to disqualify him just as Arthur walked out," which was kind of strange. So now you had a match with two losers. They couldn't award the match to Arthur so they had to hem and haw it out and the next day they decided that Arthur was the winner, and Nastase then sent roses to Arthur. They were pals actually.

❦

Willis Thomas, *Ashe's teenage doubles partner, didn't know it at the time, but he was playing with a future worldwide icon whose example guided his own actions:*

Although Ashe rarely displayed a temper, he did have strong emotions as he displays here after missing a tie-breaking point against Ken Rosewall in the semifinals of the 1972 U.S. Professional Indoor Championships. Rosewall ended up beating Ashe. (AP/Wide World Photos)

To have known somebody personally who was an icon really means something to me. Start with how he handled the AIDS thing and the trip to South Africa. That's the example for how I run the Arthur Ashe children's program here in Washington. What things I have to say about Arthur I say proudly and not just from the standpoint of his being a tennis champion, but also for his statements on issues like South Africa.

I work for an organization called the Washington Tennis and Education Foundation. There are some congresspeople on our board, and this program is a combination of tennis and education. We also have an Arthur Ashe Academy that gives kids chances to play tournaments and earn college scholarships. We are involved with nineteen schools and about four hundred kids who participate in the program, so his legacy is living on. My goal is to bring tennis out to those areas where it otherwise wouldn't have been available. It involves kids in third grade through high school, and it's a game for a lifetime. It does take a whole lot to become a champion, and a lot of that has to do with the foundation in our home. A lot of these kids don't have that strong foundation.

⌒〰〰〜∽

Robert Kelleher, Ashe's first Davis Cup captain (in 1963), offers a succinct assessment of Ashe's legacy:

It's kind of a mixed bag. He was very highly regarded for his comportment after he disclosed he had AIDS. It was against his wishes, but he took it up and went public about it. His comportment only added to his approval as a person, and his status as a champion helped him in getting his message across. I think he achieved a place and position there that will always be a great part of his legacy.

⌒〰〰〜∽

Dennis Ralston adds:

Arthur tried to make a difference while he was here, and I think he did. He tried to set a good example for all tennis players, not just his race. He was a great player. When he was on, he was unbeatable. It was just a tough thing for him with all that other stuff happening needlessly.

⌒〰〰〜∽

Seth Abraham met Ashe through tennis and television, but Abraham knew from early on that Ashe was more than just an ex-jock—much more:

Arthur did not define himself as a tennis player. It's what he did for a living and what he did extraordinarily well, and it gave him a great sense of satisfaction. But he was much more of a citizen, a citizen of the world, than merely a tennis player. So many athletes today define themselves as athletes. It's who they are, not just what they are, and that's the way it is. But Arthur had a much broader vision for himself and for the country. He had contributions that he wanted to make in this world that went well beyond just being a tennis player. Tennis was the way he earned a living, it gave him a bully pulpit, it gave him a platform, it gave him lots of things that he then used for a much bigger vision of what legacy he wanted to leave. Very few athletes have those kind of broad shoulders to do that.

Athletes do have a choice about whether or not they are role models. The way an athlete or any important person conducts themselves, even if they don't want to be a role model, they are role models because of their notoriety. Their notoriety doesn't necessarily mean deserved notoriety. You could be a bad boy or bad girl and get a lot of notoriety. I think Arthur was extraordinarily self-aware of his position as an African American, as an athlete-star, as somebody who was incredibly articulate—he kept a voluminous diary of his life experiences, although I can't tell you that he wrote in it every day, but if it wasn't every day, it was every other day. He just had much broader shoulders than just a right arm carrying a tennis racket.

∽∭∾

Adds **Donald Dell**:

His legacy is severalfold. One, he was really a thinking man's athlete. What do I mean by that? He really believed in doing it with his racket and his intellect, not his mouth. And he did it all the time. Arthur always believed that man was inherently good, much more good than bad. He was always giving people second, third, and fourth chances. He was very strong about that.

People are always talking about role models these days and you've got some of these guys saying, "No, we're not really role models, we're just out here to do our thing." It's so much b.s. It's a joke. Whether they like it or not, they are role models. They don't have to like it, they don't have to want to be it. In fact, if you're a public figure, just like if you're a United States senator or a congresswoman, you're a role model, whether you want to be or not. People look up to you, analyze you, evaluate your behavior, and or forth. But Arthur had tremendous credentials. He was a second lieutenant in the army, went to UCLA, majored in business—he was a very intelligent, smart guy. And he also happened to be a good damn athlete and he happened to be black. He won the first U.S. Open played, and he was black.

One of Ashe's causes was tennis itself, as his widow **Jeanne Moutoussamy-Ashe** *pointed out:*

Arthur was very committed to the USTA and to helping it create opportunities for those who need them most.[1]

*One of the legacies Ashe left behind was his commitment to giv-
ing more youngsters a chance to learn about sportsmanship and
life through tennis, and it was a subject that Ashe discussed at
length with* **Nick Bollettieri** *when they ran into each other at
the 1987 French Open:*

I can remember talking to Arthur when he said, "Nick, what
are we to do about the hundreds of thousands of boys and
girls who are potential champions and aren't getting the
chance to play?" And I said, "Don't worry about it, Arthur,
I'm taking care of it." We had been talking about tennis in
general and how there were so few blacks in the sport, and
how important it would be to get tennis into the recreation
centers. That would be so as to give everyone interested an
opportunity to develop their talents. I remember it as a very
nice day. I was with Andre Agassi and Jim Courier at that
time.

I knew Arthur fairly well by then. He would come to our
camp, as would other guys like Stan Smith, Charlie Pasarell,
Bob Lutz, Marty Riessen. They all came to my camp during
the summer and would work for me. That's when I really
began to know Arthur. We always had a good relationship
because I would see him a lot at tournaments and we could
talk. At that French Open in 1987, Arthur was saying, "Boy,
if some of these other kids had an opportunity to go to your
camp and get into that environment, that would really
inspire them." I said, "Arthur, I would be glad to help." I was
motivated because of the respect I had for him. It wasn't just
in what he said to me but it was in how he said it to me, spo-
ken in such a way that it motivated me. Arthur recommended a few kids he knew from different parts around the
country and then Bob Davis got involved.

Arthur never really talked about the game of tennis. He was more concerned with helping people. I can remember to the late sixties and even then he spoke about his awareness of a lack of minorities in the game, but he never talked about prejudice. What he said was that (minorities) either didn't have the opportunity or they didn't have the money. Later he came to me in the late seventies and recommended Rodney Harmon (a top-notch, up-and-coming African-American tennis player at the time) to me.

⤶⤷

Bollettieri wasn't the first to engage in a serious conversation with Ashe about the future of youths in tennis. **Chris Beck** *remembers the topic coming up more than thirty years ago:*

After he won the U.S. Open in 1968, he and another friend of my husband's and mine, Sherry Snyder, and another friend, Charlie Pasarell, who was a friend from Arthur's college days, were all talking once about how more (minority) kids could get into tennis, an all-white sport, and how would more kids have the opportunity to do what Arthur did. How could the game open more doors? He became a champion and while not everyone can, there are so many more benefits in terms of having a platform from which to speak and make a difference. Eventually, the National Junior Tennis League was created where play would take place on public courts, exposing kids to tennis. To appeal to the masses, it was devised to have brightly colored team T-shirts, giveaway rackets, and team competition. Kids get into the game by learning about winning versus losing while using Ping-Pong type scoring, and then you teach them how the game is really played and scored.

When my husband and I first found out about this concept, we got very excited and created a chapter. The first chapter had been in Harlem, New York, and ours in Philadelphia was the second or third chapter. That was 1969. As things developed and more chapters were created across the country, there was now a nonprofit umbrella that was able to oversee all these youth recreational, summertime programs. I got involved in this nonprofit organization and became president for five years, when Arthur was on the board and quite involved working with sponsors and helping the program grow.

One of the things most remarkable about him was the way he was so comfortable moving through so many different worlds all the time, and doing it very effectively. Arthur was also on Aetna's board of directors, yet he was just as comfortable with kids on the court when giving clinics in any kind of neighborhood. Then he would turn around and be at home at a party for big donors of the nonprofit organization.

People always wanted to hear what he had to say. At NJTL board meetings, he voiced his strong feelings about how to grow the program so as to offer more opportunities for the kids. One of the things I loved about him was that he would always say, "You can only do one thing at a time." He could say that in spite of the fact that he was always juggling. Now I juggle and I always think back to his saying that. He was extraordinarily articulate; understated, yes, but thoughtful and obviously very intelligent. He was a humanitarian in that he cared, and his perspective was always respected.

In 1985 the nonprofit here was given a five-court indoor tennis court. One of the conditions of the gift was that the facility would be restricted to use by children—we could not sell court time to make money. It was only for kids. Because I had known Arthur and worked with him a great deal in the NJTL, I was able to phone him and ask if he would lend his name to that center, and it is now the Arthur Ashe Youth Tennis Center, Philadelphia. Right now I'm chairing the organization looking to build an expanded indoor-outdoor Arthur Ashe Youth Tennis Center here. Our tenth benefit was to be that April after his death. Up until then he came once or twice a year to help us raise funds, to give clinics for the children, and to talk about the value of education, which was another one of his pet projects. But this is just one city and he was involved with other locales as well, such as one in California, and there's a recreation center named after him in Richmond. There are a handful of places that have the honor of bearing his name.

I think he made quite an impact because he and Charlie Pasarell and Sherry Snyder were really the first ones to say, "Hey, let's do something to make tennis more appealing to more kids. Let's go to the public parks and create viable programs in which kids can have fun playing the game right off instead of the traditional, 'First you learn a backhand, then you learn a forehand, and then you learn to serve and only then can you play the game, and win and lose.'" He was so innovative in so many ways. There is so much more focus across the country in public programming for kids than ever before and I take the position that he had a part in starting all that. He was ahead of his time in reaching out to junior masses, such as what golf is doing now with its First Tee program. Isn't that because of the impact of Tiger Woods? It made people stop and think, "What should we be doing?" Arthur Ashe transcended tennis, for sure.

◦◦◦◦◦◦◦◦

Ashe did more than just lend his name to youth tennis. He was truly a hands-on force, as **DD Eisenberg** *discovered to her delight during their years of working together for youth in the Washington, D.C., area:*

Arthur was still involved in giving me advice up until the day he died. I would call him to ask him questions about how to handle kids and how far I should go in taking some of these inner-city black kids into areas in which they had never been before, such as wealthy homes. Is that a good thing or a bad thing? Should I worry that it's a world so different from theirs that it would affect them adversely? He sort of laughed and said that he thought it was all the more important to get them out so that they could see other ways of living and could therefore develop some aspirations. Otherwise they would be stuck in their own little neighborhoods and never get out.

Arthur conducted a clinic for a lot of minority kids in Florida, giving them lessons on how to act, including etiquette on the tennis court or what to do when they would be the only black kids going into elite tennis clubs. That was very important to him. The thing that got him so excited was not so much teaching these kids the game of tennis but teaching them the game of life. Arthur didn't have a very excitable voice, but when it went up another notch, even on the telephone, I could tell that he was smiling and being very animated by his standards. One day he said, "DD, you wouldn't believe this, but today I gave a kid his first library card." He was so proud. During a tennis session at one of his programs in New Jersey, he was able to take these kids in groups to go get their library cards with their name on it. He would go to the local hospital to work out a deal where they would donate services for health prevention and health maintenance and testing, so that all these kids could get some coverage. He was always looking out for the whole person, which is something I'm trying to do now. Whenever I hear a kid say something that would have made Arthur smile, I think about him. I just know that he's looking down on all the people that he's affected. He has made an amazing difference, and hopefully it will become an endless rippling effect.

ᖗᙳᙳᖕᓄ

In praising Ashe and his legacy, **Beck** *goes back to the idea of how one man transcended his sport:*

The phrase has been used before, but Arthur was a citizen of the world. He obviously transcended tennis. He broke down so many barriers for one thing. He was very proactive and that's how he lived his life. There was the time that he went to the library to research something about African-American athletes and there wasn't a comprehensive volume on the subject, so he said, "Okay, I had better do this myself." And he devoted several years of his life to do those three volumes *(Hard Road to Glory)*. Certainly he was involved in the South African issue. He participated in life in a thoughtful, intelligent, leadership, humanitarian way.

∽

Eisenberg gives some background of her work in youth tennis and how that involved Ashe:

The Washington Tennis and Education Foundation was started in 1955 as a program to raise money for juniors so they could travel to play tournaments. One of the first players given money in this program was Donald Dell. As time went on, the mission changed and it was found that there were so many kids in the worst neighborhoods of Washington that needed help. So the Arthur Ashe Children's program was one of the big programs that was created for the purpose of going into the worst neighborhoods to clean off the courts that were filled with broken glass or whatever and run by drug lords. This was done so we could have a school-based tennis and tutoring program.

It started out as four days a week: two days of tennis and two days of tutoring. We got teachers to do the tutoring after school and paid them a stipend, and then we changed the tutoring to literacy and life skills because we realized that the tutoring as it was wasn't doing much good. So we've now developed a whole curriculum and are in nineteen public schools where we do this tennis and tutoring. That's the program that Willis runs. Then we have this stadium court where they have a once-a-year professional tournament, with some of the proceeds going to our foundation. There are all these fancy suites that surround this stadium that seats seventy-five hundred, and we have another twenty-four to thirty courts right outside the stadium. After we have this professional tournament, we then open up the stadium and all the tennis courts for clinics and youth tournaments. After school we have literacy programs, college-prep programs and computer labs. There's a whole other group of kids we are reaching in this other neighborhood in the northwest with a lot of Hispanic and African-American kids.

We touch the life of the whole person just like what Arthur always wanted to do. We're making a difference and in many cases saving lives by taking kids out of the street and into a program in which tennis is the carrot to get them interested, and then we hit them with a heavy dose of education. Some of the kids are terrible tennis players and will never make it in tennis, but they are staying in school and coming in after school, and we're tracking them so we can know what they're doing and see where certain kids need tutoring in certain areas. A lot of these kids now are thinking about college that would never have thought about it otherwise.

Even though most of these kids don't know who Arthur Ashe is, part of our curriculum is Arthur Ashe and we look at him through history with books and stuff. We read of his travels as well as the books he wrote. So his name is very much in the middle of things. We also have something called the Arthur Ashe Reading and Fundamental Room and there are only about five of these in the country. They are dedicated to reading. We have a complete library, so believe me, his legacy lives on and on. You see it every day.

❧

Frank Deford, *Ashe's co-author of* Portrait in Motion *and another of Ashe's good friends, recalls how Ashe showed his true colors as a man who wouldn't be ruled by bitterness even in the face of an obvious health-care mistake that ultimately cost him his life:*

After doing the book with him, I continued to see Arthur over the years for the rest of his life. It wasn't just a matter of being journalist-subject, the book is over, and now we go our separate ways. When he had his (first) heart attack, which was really the beginning of the end for Arthur, I got *Sports Illustrated* to do an article on him, and people were pretty astonished because he was only thirty-six years old. By the time I got to the hospital, he had been in around three or four days and already he was an expert on the heart. Just like a doctor. That's another example of how he would get ahold of a subject and absolutely swallow it. He really knew all about heart attacks. It was the second heart attack when they told him, "Look, why don't you get a blood transfusion. You don't need it, but if you get it, it will really get you going." It was sort of a simple choice to be made, but as it turns out that's when he got the bad blood. If it had been about a year and a half later, which by that time they had started testing the blood, they would have found out that it was bad blood and he never would have gotten AIDS. Yet, he was wonderful about that. People would say, "Why don't you sue the hospital?" and he would say, "Look, it's really not anybody's fault; it's just one of those things." It was bad luck. One never could have been more placid. He never complained. That was the way life had made him a tennis champion and life had done this to him, too.

⌒∞⌒

Rodney Harmon remembers Ashe as much for his modesty and humility as anything, starting with how Ashe carried himself in public—not insulated by entourages and almost always on time:

On thing I remember about him is a clinic that we had in Miami. By then I was working for the USTA as a national coach and Arthur had helped me with a recommendation when I first went to work for the USTA. He had been the pro at Doral for a while. We were both with Head, which was sponsoring the clinic. About ten minutes before the workshop we couldn't find Arthur anywhere. We didn't know where he was and we had people waiting for this thing to start. Everyone was wondering if someone was supposed to pick him up or take care of him or whatever, and then all of a sudden he just comes walking across the street with no entourage or anything like that. He was just by himself, and it said a lot about him being a guy who didn't want others making a big deal out of him, when everyone else was running around freaking with our heads cut off. But he was always very punctual and he knew he wasn't going to be late.

Then to watch him with the children—that was really something. He had taken the time to prepare a short speech, when a lot of times you get people at those things who aren't really prepared; they just wing it. He took time to try and hit balls with each of the kids, and what really impressed me was how he would try to make every kid at the clinic feel important. He had a lot of knowledge and would do things for the kids. He really took extra time and, finally, he stayed so long we told him that he probably needed to go for the sake of his own busy schedule because he was still out there after the clinic was supposed to end hitting balls with the kids, giving tips, and stuff like that. Some kids would ask him about his tennis tournaments, so he would stop and talk about that, or they would ask him about his trip to South Africa, so he would stop and talk about that, too. It was kind of a funny thing to see this, to see him in action in that kind of environment with the children, because he absolutely loved children.

⊙~~~◎

Harry Marmion, *a USTA president at one time, had this to say about Ashe and his legacy:*

Arthur Ashe was an outstanding tennis player, but we are naming our new stadium in his honor because he was the finest human being the sport of tennis has ever known. Arthur was—and through the example he set, still is—a role model to people throughout the world. It is only fitting that we recognize one of the brightest stars of tennis's past through the facility that will be the focus of tennis's future.[2]

⊙~~~◎

Added writer **Kenny Moore:**

It was his consciousness that stayed with you. When he turned his open, bespectacled, deceptively tranquil gaze upon an event or an argument, it got turned over and over in a blazing tungsten light. But this was an illumination shaded by all the elements of the Ashe consciousness, the capacity of an information junkie to equal the complexity of the world, sort it out, deal with the worst of it, fix it and see the way on.[3]

⊙~~~◎

Jeanne Moutoussamy-Ashe added this epitaph for her deceased husband:

He fought hard, and as in his tennis days, it was always how he played the game.[4]

❧

Stan Smith offers the consummate explanation of what made Ashe's legacy so special:

Arthur wasn't a Jackie Robinson in that sense of being the first African American in a sport's premier competitive organization—Althea Gibson was. But he certainly will be thought of whenever people think of black pioneers in tennis. His leadership roles in the ATP (Association of Tennis Professionals) were testament to that. He helped fashion the game into what it is today. He was actually responsible for the ATP's Code of Conduct. He was committee chairman for that issue, went around and solicited input, and then wrote the basic Code of Conduct.

Worldwide, he made a huge impact as an ambassador for tennis and for the United States, not so much as a statesman but as a great role model. He was all about playing fair and playing things on the up and up without much gamesmanship. He would kind of let his racket do his talking on the court. I remember him walking off the court in a match against (Ilie) Nastase in the finals in Stockholm after Nastase had thrown a tantrum and done some sort of stall thing. Arthur told the umpire, "I'm not going to play if he's going to do this," and the umpire defaulted Nastase, and then they kind of reinstated him. It was an interesting time. Arthur was strong in his beliefs for sportsmanship on the court. He was all for playing hard, playing fair, and keeping your mouth shut.

∽☒☒☒∾

NOTES

THE VIRGINIAN

1. Moore, Kenny, "The Eternal Example," *Sports Illustrated*, December 21, 1992, p. 16.

2. Ibid.

TENNIS ACE

1. Deford, Frank, "Service, but First a Smile," *Sports Illustrated*, August 29, 1966.

2. Moore, Kenny, "He Did All He Could," *Sports Illustrated*, February 15, 1993, p. 12.

3. Ashe, Arthur, and Arnold Rampersad, *Days of Grace: A Memoir*. New York: Ballantine Books, 1994, p. 110.

BLACK AND WHITE

1. Deford, Frank, "Lessons from a Friend," *Newsweek*, February 22, 1993, p. 60.

2. Moore, Kenny, "He Did All He Could," *Sports Illustrated*, February 15, 1993, p. 12.

3. Bernstein, Peter, "Grand Slam," *U.S. News and World Report*, February 22, 1993.

4. Moore, Kenny, "The Eternal Example," *Sports Illustrated*, December 21, 1992, p. 16.

5. Ibid.

6. Ibid.

7. Witteman, Paul A., "A Man of Fire and Grace," *Time*, February 15, 1993, p. 70.

8. Moore, Kenny, "The Eternal Example," *Sports Illustrated*, December 21, 1992, p. 16.

TRUSTING FRIEND

1. Deford, Frank, "Service, but First a Smile," *Sports Illustrated*, August 29, 1966.

2. Ibid.

3. Jennings, Jay, "Arthur Ashe: Lessons from a Noble Life," *Biography*, May 1998.

CITIZEN OF THE WORLD

1. Bernstein, Peter, "Grand Slam," *U.S. News and World Report*, February 22, 1993.

2. Price, S. L., "Slow Train to Eminence," *Sports Illustrated*, September 19, 1994.

3. Moore, Kenny, "He Did All He Could," *Sports Illustrated*, February 15, 1993, p. 12.

THE LEGACY

1. "In Memory of Arthur Ashe," *Black Enterprise*, September 1997, p. 176.

2. Ibid.

3. Moore, Kenny, "He Did All He Could," *Sports Illustrated*, February 15, 1993, p. 12.

INDEX

ABOUT THE AUTHOR

Mike Towle is a veteran sportswriter and author whose previous books include *The Ultimate Golf Trivia Book, I Remember Ben Hogan,* and *I Remember Walter Payton.* A former newspaper reporter, he has written for the *Fort Worth Star-Telegram* and *The National.* Towle is president and publisher of TowleHouse Publishing Company, based in Nashville, Tennessee, where he lives with his wife, Holley, and their son, Andrew.

Printed in the USA
CPSIA information can be obtained
at www.ICGtesting.com
JSHW082148140824
68134JS00002B/37